HOW TO FIND YOUR
SIDE HUSTLE
Finding the Best Fit Side Hustle

JASON SCHMITT

ISBN: 979-8-89316-601-9 - eBook
ISBN: 979-8-89316-602-6 - Paperback
ISBN: 979-8-89316-603-3 - Hardcover

FREE
30-Minute
Introductory Meeting
with Jason!

Unlock Your Full Potential

Introducing **Our Accountability Partner Program**—your personal guide to staying motivated, achieving your goals, and growing your business.

Ready to Elevate Your Business?

Meet with Jason and discover how the Accountability Partner Program can help you reach your full potential.

Don't wait!
Take the first step toward success today!

FIREWATCH BUSINESS
BELIEVE - ACT - SUCCEED

Schedule
your
Appointment
TODAY

READY TO DISCOVER YOUR PASSION?

Start your journey to a more fulfilled life today. Download your FREE Passion Questionnaire now and take the first step toward doing what you love.

What's Inside?

- **Identify What You Love:** Uncover your true interests and passions.

- **Narrow Down Options:** Focus on careers, businesses, or side hustles that align with your passions.

- **Live with Purpose:** Find a path that brings joy and meaning to your life.

- **Make a Difference:** Choose work that not only fulfills you but also positively impacts others.

Find Your True Calling with Our Free Passion Questionnaire!

Are you searching for a career, business, or side hustle that truly excites you? Imagine waking up every day to do something you love—something that not only fulfills you but also makes a difference in the world.

FIREWATCH BUSINESS
Your Partner from Progress to Accomplishment

CONTENTS

INTRODUCTION

First, ask yourself about your primary financial goal for the future. It doesn't matter what your current situation is, whether you are single, married, a student, a full-time employer, a businessperson, or whatever. Just evaluate your current financial position and financial obligations. Do you think that you can achieve the above-mentioned financial goals? Are you confident enough to manage your income and expenses in the current economic situation? This evaluation will help you understand your financial status and whether you can have an early retirement or financial freedom in the future.

An American businessperson and investor, Warren Buffet, once said, "If you don't find a way to make money while you sleep, you will work until you die" (Barker, 2021). As he emphasized, it's important to develop additional income streams apart from your day job. That will determine whether you'll be able to reach financial freedom sooner or later. However, it's important to note that if you prefer to work hard until your last breath, that's perfectly fine too.

Nevertheless, this book is specifically for those who want to start their own side hustle and maximize their earnings to achieve their dream life in the near future. So, let's first understand what a side hustle is. A side hustle is an additional employment opportunity that brings in extra money beyond one's regular or full-time job. A side hustle differs from a part-time job as it offers more flexibility and autonomy in the tasks you undertake.

I personally believe having multiple income streams is wise, as it allows you to weather economic changes more effectively. With just a single income, it's difficult to live the life you want. This is why a growing number of full-time employed adults, especially young people, are turning toward side hustles. In fact, recent statistics show that 34% of Americans already have a side hustle (Zhou, 2024).

The younger generation, specifically millennials, have more side hustles than their older counterparts. This is due in part to the college debt and affordability housing crisis that forced many of them to find additional sources of income. The U.S. side hustle market value is around $2.58 trillion, and Americans who dedicate an average of just 12 hours per week make over $13,000 per year (Zhou, 2024).

There are numerous benefits associated with starting a side hustle. Many individuals start a side hustle based on their passion and turn it into an income source. This provides the opportunity to do something you love and earn extra cash, which improves cash flow, financial stability, and security. During the COVID-19 pandemic, many people lost their primary jobs, but those with extra sources of income were able to survive. Having a side hustle also provides a safety net in case you need to make a career change, as your income won't be completely cut off.

Moreover, a passive income source like a side hustle also creates a little breathing room to start saving and planning for the future, reducing any financial stress. In contrast to a regular 9-to-5 job, a side hustle allows you to set your own work hours and have complete control over your work. Income from a side hustle can be used to pay off debt quickly, especially high-interest credit cards. Committing to a full-time job can be a challenge to figure out your creative side, but with a side hustle, you can utilize your free time to create a better version of yourself.

Switching from a traditional job to self-employment through a side hustle can improve your mental health as well as self-confidence. It's a great opportunity to learn new skills, meet new people, and expand your network. When you work on your side hustle, you have more responsibilities and need to allocate more time, which eventually helps you improve your time management skills. A successful side hustle also creates more opportunities for others, which is a benefit for everyone. Ultimately, seeing your small business grow or getting paid for a service or product you created gives you a sense of satisfaction, accomplishment, and pride.

Side hustles come with their own set of challenges. One of the most difficult aspects is finding a profitable and sustainable idea, which can consume a lot of time and effort. Starting a side hustle means managing and balancing multiple responsibilities and time, which can be even more challenging with the demands of a regular job and other commitments. While some side hustle owners can put in double the time and effort as compared to a regular job, their energy levels can dwindle over time.

Starting a side hustle also requires a financial investment, which can be a major challenge for many individuals. Taking on some level of risk is inevitable, and there is a possibility of not being successful, which can affect the expected earnings. Getting the support of others, especially investors, can be another pressure.

With time, the pace of the side hustle can feel frustrating, and the joy of the gig can fade. Initially, these challenges can be daunting, but the benefits of starting a side hustle are exceptional. Based on my years of experience, I can guide you step-by-step to start your side hustle and overcome any challenges that come your way, and even how to turn them into opportunities.

Before we proceed with the other chapters, let me share my journey with you. I have always been an entrepreneur and grew up with my parents, who owned several successful businesses. I learned from an early age that dedication and hard work pay off. When I started my own side hustle, I invested $3000. In the second year, I earned $21,000, and in the third year, I earned $30,000. This is only a bit of my success story. I have all the knowledge and equipment to direct you to become a successful side hustle owner. From finding a business idea to scaling your side hustle, I cover every important stage. It's time to turn to Chapter 1, and I hope you'll enjoy each section. Good luck!

CHAPTER 1

Understanding Your Motivation

Have you made a decision about starting your own side hustle after weighing the pros and cons? Peter F. Drucker, a management consultant, educator, and author, once stated, "Whenever you see a successful business, someone once made a courageous decision" ("100+ Small Business Quotes," n.d.). To succeed in business, you must first have the determination to start and grow while overcoming the fear of failure or risk. One thing to keep in mind is that there is no straight line to success in business. I agree with you that taking the first step may be challenging, but it is essential to change your life. So, in this section, let me assist you in finding the motivation and personal goals to start a side hustle. Let's get started by discussing the importance of having multiple income streams or developing new skills.

IMPORTANCE OF HAVING MULTIPLE INCOME STREAMS AND SKILLS DEVELOPMENT

Before we begin, let me ask you a question: how many sources of income do you have? Can you rely on just one? Given the current economic situation, it can be difficult to depend on a single income stream. That's why it's better to have multiple income streams. Here are the main types of income streams:

- **Active income:** You can earn active income through a job by exchanging your time and energy for wages, salaries, tips, and commissions. It requires you to be actively involved to earn income, so side hustles also fall under this category.

- **Passive income:** In this case, you're not necessarily too involved. Examples of passive income include renting properties, affiliate marketing, starting a YouTube channel or blog, writing an e-book, and so on.

- **Portfolio income:** You can earn this income through investments such as dividends, interest, royalties, and capital gains. Examples include investing in stocks, high-yield CD or savings accounts, and peer-to-peer lending.

Having multiple income streams increases your overall earning potential, allowing you to achieve your financial goals faster. Once you exceed your income target, you can reinvest in different investments and savings accounts, accumulate assets, and increase your wealth, financial independence, greater financial stability, and security. Multiple income streams are a good risk mitigation strategy, providing you with more freedom and flexibility. If you lose your main source of income, you have the freedom to rely on your secondary income during turbulent times.

Different income streams are an excellent way to explore different interests, develop skills, and improve your creativity, knowledge, and innovation, resulting in enhanced personal and professional growth. Knowing that you're not solely reliant on one paycheck or one income stream reduces your financial stress and provides peace of mind. So, if you are smart and manage more than one source of income, trust me, you can live your dream life.

I believe that with further skills development, you can have many sources of income. For example, improving your cooking skills can lead to starting your own restaurant or food truck. Skills development also helps personal and professional improvement. Basically, skills development means improving certain skills to be more efficient and effective. When it comes to the workplace, there are three types of skill development: upskilling, cross-skilling, and reskilling. Upskilling means improving your skills for your current role, while cross-skilling means learning new skills for your current role. Reskilling means learning new skills to move to a new role. To enhance your skills, follow the steps below:

- **Overcome your fears:** For instance, if you have a fear of speaking in front of others, this will stop you and prevent you from speaking in public even when the need arises. So, identify any areas that you are scared of improving, take the necessary steps to overcome them, and boost your confidence.

- **Believe in yourself:** When you are confident, you dare to handle any stressful situations or challenges. It will not be easy, and you will have setbacks, but a belief in yourself will allow you to get back to working toward the goal and handle any stressful situations or challenges. So, always think positively.

- **Think about your goal and identify your skills gap:** If you have a desire to start your own coffee shop, then you need to improve skills that are particularly needed for a Barista as well as restaurant management. Let's say you have most of them, but your customer management skills need to be improved. Therefore, establish goals, accordingly, and determine where you need improvement.

- **Target-specific skill areas:** Skills can be mainly divided into two categories including soft skills and technical skills. Soft skills include creativity, communication, time management, teamwork, and so on while technical skills include specific abilities which are required to perform complex tasks. Based on your goals, determine what type of skill set you need to improve.

- **Expand your network:** Networking is one of the best methods to improve your skills. If you wish to improve yourself as a Barista, then you can join social media pages, industrial events, forums, and other communities. There, you'll be able to meet and interact with various categories of people, seek support, and form formidable partnerships that can benefit you in the future. Also, don't think twice about seeking feedback from others, even your family members. Ask them to observe particular skills and share their honest feedback. Accordingly, you can determine what areas you did well and where you underperformed.

- **Get a coach or a mentor:** It's a good idea to contact a professional who has considerable experience and is in a higher position than you. For example, a manager, supervisor, professor, consultant, or expert in the same field you are in. This approach may be more expensive but may help your bottom line in the long run.

- **Read and research:** Read and learn as much as possible. Resources are abundant both in print and online. So, get the maximum benefit out of them to improve your comprehension regarding any skills. Watching videos could be another more engaging learning method that keeps you updated and informed about recent trends.

- **Take courses and undergo training:** Some platforms and organizations offer training programs and courses for free. Research them and consider signing up.

- **Seek certification:** There can be situations where you need to prove your skills to others. Therefore, it's better to seek courses and training programs that offer certificates.

- **Practice:** The more you practice a skill, the better you'll become at it. Apply the skills you've learned to your daily life and enhance them further.

- **Adapt to change:** Changes are inevitable. So, be flexible and adaptable to cope with any changes that come your way.

In this section, we understood the importance of having multiple sources of income and how to enhance your skills. Now, it's time to discover why you need to start a side hustle. Let's move to the next section.

> **"You don't have to be great to start, but you have to start to be great."**
>
> Zig Ziglar

Identifying Personal Goals and Motivations for a Side Hustle

After understanding the benefits of having multiple sources of income, I hope many of you are now willing to start your own side hustle. There are many reasons why individuals might want to begin a side hustle beyond just earning extra money. Remember, it always starts with why—Who are you doing this for? Likewise, it's important to understand your goals and motivations for starting a side hustle so you can maintain momentum over the long term. Here are some common motivators for a successful side hustle.

- **Earn extra money and increase financial security:** This is one of the most common reasons to start a side hustle. If you're struggling to save money for your future goals, then a side hustle can be a great way to earn extra income. Additionally, having a side hustle means you have a backup plan if something happens to your main source of income. On the other hand, recent studies show that 79% of employees in the age group of 25 to 44 are unhappy with their current jobs and want to leave them (Ghosh, 2021). I am not sure whether you also fall into this category. Don't worry about the time you gave away from your employer that you can't get back. This is the right time to sell your time and effort for your own venture and yourself. In addition to these, a side hustle can be a way to achieve your dreams and reach your goals. Whether you want to pay off debt, save for a down payment on a house, or travel the world, a side hustle can help you get there.

- **You probably have more time than you think:** For many people, time is the main excuse not to start a side hustle. It can be true for individuals who work 9-5 jobs, manage household chores, and take care of their children when they get home. These kinds of cases are legitimate, but still, I'd argue many of you do have the time to start a side hustle. Let me explain why I am saying you might have more time than you think. Do you know an average person spends 1,300 hours per year and 3.5 hours per day on social media alone (Hoyt, 2023)? What about you—How many hours do you spend on social media per day? Can you cut at least one hour of your social media usage and put it toward a side hustle? I know many of you are wondering how side-hustling one hour a day will help you. Am I correct? I have an answer for that as well! There are many small yet lucrative side hustle options. One of my friends does ride-sharing on his way home from work. I know many college students who work as freelance writers who just write a few words per day and earn a few hundred dollars as their pocket money. Last week, I spoke with one of my nieces who does dog walking for half an hour every day for her neighbors and earns a considerable amount per week. This may seem insignificant at first, but it can lead to greater opportunities in the future.

- **You are earning way less than your potential:** Imagine you are working as a software engineer for a leading IT company. Don't you think that you have the capacity to start online IT classes for college students or deliver IT solutions online? Another example: Assume you are working as an architect, but you are a very good singer. Unfortunately, you haven't used your passion to generate an income. So, side hustles are a great opportunity to make use of your untapped skills or passion. Right after work or on weekends, you can perform at a restaurant with your singing talent. Does this sound great?

- **Starting a side hustle is achievable for anyone:** Unlike other income sources, there's something for any and every one in a side hustle. For many of the side hustle ideas, you don't need a high level of education or expertise to get started. However, do keep in mind that, as I emphasized earlier, developing your skills can help you access more opportunities. The main skills you need in side hustles are motivation, dedication, and the right mindset. If you think that you can, yes, you can. The first step can be challenging but believe in yourself. Once you've got your reason for side hustling—it can be anything to generate income or utilize your skills—you can start making things happen.

Many successful business owners started their business as a side hustle without anticipating it would become their full-time job. I wouldn't say turning your side hustle into your main source of income is not a risk. For example, income might not be as steady in the beginning, and you may have to invest more time and effort to make it a success. Don't you think it is highly rewarding and worthwhile to take risks for your own success instead of someone else's? Let me remind you that hard work pays off! Don't be the person who wishes they started a side hustle earlier. Start making money now; if you don't start one, someone else will. Some may say that a side income may not make you a multi-millionaire, but we never know what our destiny holds. All you need is initiative and a strong desire to succeed.

Famous Businesses That Started Out as Side Hustles

I hope now you have found a valid reason and are motivated to start your own side hustle. Here is another boost, and in this section, we discuss various successful business owners who started as side hustles. Can you believe that the co-founders of **Apple**, Steve Jobs and Steve

Wozniak, built a computer in a garage as a side project, and later it became Apple I? Similarly, **Facebook** started as a dorm room side project of its co-founders, Mark Zuckerberg, Dustin Moskovitz, Eduardo Saverin, and Chris Hughes. In 2003, Zuckerberg developed Facemash for Harvard University students. Though it was not successful, his friends were inspired by that project. As a result, in 2004, they created a social networking site called Facebook for Harvard students, and eventually, it expanded to colleges all over the country and outside of college life. As of the third quarter of 2023, Facebook had 3.05 billion monthly active users, making it the largest app in the world (Shepherd, 2024).

Instagram was a side project for its founder, Kevin Systrom. Apart from his day job, Kevin was teaching himself how to code and eventually built a more picture-based mobile check-in app called Burbn. Later, he quit his day job, raised $500,000, and hired his co-founder, Mike Krieger. As a result of both of their hard work, Instagram was officially launched in 2010, and they had only 100,000 users in the first week. As of January 2024, Instagram recorded 2.4 billion active users, making it one of the top five social networking platforms globally, and they are estimated to reach over 2.5 billion by the end of 2024 (Ruby, 2024).

Can you believe that the famous scented candle company **Yankee Candle** was once a teenager's side hustle? Mike Kittredge used to make handcrafted candles in his kitchen, and in 1969, when he was only 16 years old, he gifted one of his candles to his mom. One of his neighbors saw it and asked Mike to make another candle for him for $2, and it was the turning point in his life. After that, he started making candles as a side hustle. He operated out of his parent's garage and basement. He expanded his business, and in 1998, he sold it for $500 million. At present, Yankee Candle has hundreds of stores all around the world (Olito, 2020).

Innocent Drinks, a company that produces smoothies and juice, was founded by university graduates in 1998 while they were working full-time. Their aim was to create healthy smoothies. After some time, they sold their products at a festival and asked customers to put their empty bottles into two bins labeled "yes" and "no," seeking feedback on whether they should continue their business. They were pleasantly surprised when the answer was a resounding yes, which led them to quit their day jobs. In 2009, the company sold a minority stake to The Coca-Cola Company for £30 million, and currently, Coca-Cola owns over 90% of the company (Bergman, 2019).

Airbnb is another example of how a small side hustle can lead to huge success. In 2017, Airbnb founders Joe Gebbia and Brian Chesky were struggling to pay rent as housemates in San Francisco. They placed air mattresses in their living room and marketed them as a bed and breakfast for a big conference. Eventually, their former roommate, Nathan Blecharczyk, became the third co-founder of their new venture, which they named AirBed & Breakfast. They launched a website and began offering short-term living quarters and breakfast for those who couldn't afford a hotel room. In 2009, they shortened the company name to Airbnb.com and started listing entire rooms and properties. As of January 2024, Airbnb has a market cap of $89.68 billion and is available in more than 220 countries worldwide (Airbnb, Inc., n.d.).

Udemy, a prominent education technology company, was founded by Eren Bali, who worked as a freelance web developer. While working for various clients, he dedicated extra effort and funds to his own passion project. In 2007, he developed software for a live virtual classroom. In 2010, with the help of co-founders Gagan Biyani and Oktay Caglar, he launched Udemy. As of June 2023, Udemy has over 64 million learners and more than 75,000 instructors and offers over 210,000 courses in nearly 75 languages (*Udemy*, 2024).

As you can see, the majority of successful businesses were started as a side hustle or a side project. Don't you think you have the same potential to reach the same level? Yes, you can, and have faith in yourself!

Before we move on to the next chapter, let's do a small activity. Grab a pen and paper, and list the reasons why you need to start a side hustle. The second activity is to read more successful stories of individuals who turned their side hustle into a huge business and note the turning points of their lives and the steps they took differently compared to others. Once you complete these two activities, you are good to turn to the next page.

CHAPTER 2

Unveiling Your Skills and Passions

I want to remind you of the previous chapter, where we discussed your motivations for starting a side hustle. Now, it's time to identify the specific skills and passions that could be beneficial for your side hustle. As we discussed in the previous section, skill development is crucial to increase your opportunities for success. However, if you lack a particular skill, it's essential to become an expert to sell yourself or your product. Don't worry; we will conduct a self-assessment to determine potential side hustles based on your existing skills and interests. To begin with, we will provide you with the necessary resources to identify your skills and hobbies that you can market. Additionally, we'll discuss the scalability and sustainability of different side hustles to help you make an informed decision about the best one for you.

CONDUCTING A SELF-ASSESSMENT

Aspiring entrepreneurs must first understand their personal needs, strengths, personality traits, skills, talents, and interests to make informed decisions when starting a side hustle. There are several ways to determine these factors, ranging from making lists to taking various tests, including:

- **Value evaluations:** This test takes into account factors such as the salary or income level you desire, your preference for frequent interactions with others at work, how much you want your work to contribute to society, and how important prestige is to your work and your life.

- **Interest evaluations:** These tests collect data on your likes and dislikes concerning people, activities, and objects.

- **Personality evaluations:** These tests are often used in online surveys and categorize individuals into 16 personality types, such as introversion or extroversion, judging or perceiving, and so forth. In reality, individuals with particular personality types perform certain tasks better than others. For example, extroverted people enjoy working with other people, and they have higher engagement levels than introverted people.

- **Aptitude evaluations:** This kind of test evaluates your abilities and strengths and suggests whether you need more training, education, time, effort, or money for your next step in life, for example starting a new career.

You may use any of the above methods to analyze yourself and identify the right side hustle for you. Additionally, I have attached two self-assessment questionnaires to further ease your decision.

Self-Assessment Questionnaire

1. What activities make you lose track of time when you're doing them?
2. If money were no object, how would you spend your time?
3. What topics or subjects can you talk about for hours without getting bored?
4. What were your favorite hobbies or activities as a child?
5. What dreams or aspirations did you have when you were younger?
6. When do you feel most energized and alive?
7. If you had a free day with no obligations, how would you choose to spend it?
8. What problems in the world or your community do you feel most passionate about solving?
9. What activities bring you a sense of fulfillment and satisfaction?
10. What kind of books, movies, or documentaries do you find most inspiring or interesting?
11. When you browse the internet, what topics or content do you find yourself gravitating toward?
12. If you could learn any skill or take up any hobby, what would it be?
13. What activities make you forget to check your phone or the time?
14. Reflect on a moment in your life when you felt the most proud or accomplished—what were you doing?
15. What are my strengths and talents? - Consider the things you excel at naturally.
16. What topics or subjects do I enjoy learning about?
17. What do I daydream about?
18. What activities give me a sense of accomplishment?
19. What social or environmental issues do I care about?
20. If I could have any job or lifestyle, what would it be?

21. What feedback have I received from others about my skills or interests?
22. What challenges am I willing to face for the sake of fulfillment?
23. What skills do you possess that others might find valuable?
24. Are there any problems in your community that you could solve?
25. What are your favorite books, movies, or TV shows? Can you turn those interests into a business?
26. What are some challenges you've overcome in your life? Could you help others facing similar challenges?
27. Do you have any unique talents or abilities?
28. Are there trends or emerging industries that interest you?
29. What are your favorite online platforms or social media channels? Can you create content or services for those platforms?
30. What are the most common questions people ask you for advice on?
31. Have you identified any gaps in the market?
32. What are your favorite types of products or services to buy? Can you create something similar?
33. Have you ever thought, "I wish there was a better way to do this"? What was it, and can you create a solution?
34. What are your favorite websites or blogs? Can you contribute content to those spaces?
35. Do you enjoy working with your hands? Are there craft or DIY projects you could turn into a business?
36. What are the biggest pain points in your daily life? Can you create a service or product to address them?
37. What industries or markets do you have expertise in?
38. Are there any skills you've been wanting to learn that could be turned into a business?
39. Have you identified any trends in your current job that could lead to a side hustle opportunity?
40. What are your favorite apps? Can you create a similar, improved version?

41. Are there products or services that you wished existed but can't find on the market?
42. Do you enjoy teaching or explaining things to others? Can you create tutorials or courses?
43. What are your favorite outdoor activities? Can you turn them into a business?
44. Do you have a strong network or community that you could leverage for a business?
45. What are your favorite podcasts? Can you create content in a similar niche?
46. Have you ever freelanced or consulted in a specific area? Could you turn that into a side business?
47. Are there subscription services you use and enjoy? Can you create something similar?
48. What are your favorite types of events to attend? Can you organize similar events?
49. Are there any cultural or local trends you could tap into?
50. What are your favorite types of technology or gadgets? Can you create accessories or complementary products?
51. What are your favorite cuisines or foods? Can you create a food-related business?
52. Are there local businesses or services that are lacking in your area?
53. What are your favorite fitness activities? Can you offer services or products related to fitness?
54. Do you have expertise in a particular software or tool that others might find useful?
55. What are your favorite charities or causes? Can you create a business that supports them?
56. Have you ever won awards or accolades for something? Can you turn that skill or talent into a business?
57. Are there any government regulations or policies that could create a business opportunity?

58. What are your favorite social issues or causes? Can you create a business that promotes social good?
59. What are your favorite travel destinations? Can you create a business related to travel?
60. Do you have any connections in industries that interest you? Can you leverage those connections for a side hustle?
61. What are your financial goals, and how could a side hustle help you achieve them?

It always starts with why!

Self-Assessment Questionnaire for Small Business Readiness

Follow the below rating when answering the statements.

- 1 - Very Unlikely
- 2 - Unlikely
- 3 - Neutral
- 4 - Likely
- 5 - Very Likely

Adaptability:

- I am comfortable with change and can adapt to unforeseen circumstances.
  - 1 | 2 | 3 | 4 | 5

Risk Tolerance:

- I am willing to take calculated risks to achieve my goals.
  - 1 | 2 | 3 | 4 | 5

Time Management:

- I am effective at managing my time and priorities.
  - 1 | 2 | 3 | 4 | 5

Financial Literacy:

- I have a good understanding of basic financial concepts (budgeting, cash flow, etc.).
  - 1 | 2 | 3 | 4 | 5

Problem-Solving Skills:

- I can identify and solve problems independently.
  - 1 | 2 | 3 | 4 | 5

Networking Abilities:

- I am comfortable networking and building professional relationships.
  - 1 | 2 | 3 | 4 | 5

Self-Motivation:

- I am driven and can stay motivated even in challenging times.
  - 1 | 2 | 3 | 4 | 5

Communication Skills:

- I can effectively communicate my ideas and thoughts.
  - 1 | 2 | 3 | 4 | 5

Market Awareness:

- I have a good understanding of the market I want to enter.
  - 1 | 2 | 3 | 4 | 5

Customer Focus:

- I am committed to providing excellent customer service.
  - 1 | 2 | 3 | 4 | 5

Leadership Skills:

- I can lead and inspire a team.
  - 1 | 2 | 3 | 4 | 5

Emotional Resilience:

- I can handle setbacks and disappointments without losing focus.
  - 1 | 2 | 3 | 4 | 5

Scoring:

- 60-48: You demonstrate strong entrepreneurial potential.
- 47-36: You have the potential to start a small business with further development.
- 35-24: Consider working on certain skills before venturing into entrepreneurship.
- Below 24: Entrepreneurship may not be the best fit right now; consider further skill development or seek guidance.

Remember, this questionnaire is just a starting point for self-reflection. Entrepreneurship involves ongoing learning and adaptation, so even if you don't score high in every area, it doesn't mean you can't develop those skills over time.

How to Identify Marketable Skills or Hobbies

After completing the above activities, how do you feel? I am sure many of you might be wondering about your potential and capabilities. Also, please don't be disappointed if you scored below 24 on the second questionnaire. Trust me, this section will help you to boost your confidence and discover new skills or side hustle ideas.

Now, it's time to filter the skills you identified in the previous section and focus on identifying the most marketable ones. Evaluating how your skills align with market demands can help you turn your strengths into a source of income. It's always beneficial to do what you're good at without any pressure, and there's a saying that goes, "If you're good at something, never do it for free." Now, this is your turn to earn from what you're capable of!

To begin, let's differentiate between knowledge and skills. Knowledge refers to the information you learn through books, school, and other media, while skills are the practical application of that knowledge. However, anyone can gain knowledge, but some people will naturally be more skilled because of their natural ability. For example, you can study an architecture course and become an architect, but some individuals are naturally good at designing, and they have an "eye" for it.

Now, it's time to identify the difference between skills and talent. Imagine a group of friends taking a baking course. Everyone received the same knowledge and learned and practiced the same skills. Some of them quit baking, but others applied that theoretical knowledge to practical skills and made cakes. Do you think everyone's creations will be the same? No, at least one person's cake will likely be better tasting, structured, and designed because they have a natural talent for making cakes. Also, that person will excel in their talents and might open a cafe. To succeed in a side hustle, it's important to have a combination of knowledge, skills, and talent. Therefore, list down your own skills, knowledge, and talents separately.

After that, go through the list with a critical eye and identify the skills, knowledge, and talents that other people might want to pay you for. Look at your list to see if it can answer the following questions: Is there anything I can turn into a business? How can I solve people's needs with these skills, hobbies, knowledge, and talents?

Next, write down the side hustle ideas that you are interested in based on the short-listed skills, hobbies, knowledge, and talents. If you're unsure if you have marketable skills, don't worry. As we discussed in the previous section, you can acquire and develop new skills. These steps might take a few hours, and they are all about brainstorming but worth attempting. Here is a list of skills that you can think of learning and developing when you have a wish to start a side hustle:

- search engine optimization (SEO)
- web design
- social media skills (ex: staying updated on digital trends and learning new platforms).
- coding
- graphic design
- content writing
- content editing
- project management
- public speaking

- bookkeeping
- data analysis
- cloud computing
- artificial intelligence
- customer relationship management
- user experience
- sales
- budgeting
- human resources
- writing
- photography
- illustration and design
- podcasting
- gaming
- cooking
- gardening
- DIY crafts

As you can see, some of these skills are equally important for anyone, regardless of the type of side hustle. For example, if you started a clothing business, in addition to sewing, you would need to have social media skills to promote your business on social media platforms. To gain brand awareness for your business, you should have at least basic photography skills to capture your products and share them with your potential customers. To effectively handle your finances, it's better to have knowledge in bookkeeping, data analysis, and budgeting. Similarly, someone who has a catering business must have the same skills we've discussed earlier in addition to cooking. Having a side hustle means not mastering one particular skill. Instead, it could be a combination of skills, knowledge, and talents.

Apart from the general skills, let's discover some skills that are essential for entrepreneurs to become successful business owners. These skills include:

- business management skills
- teamwork and leadership skills
- strategic thinking and planning skills
- time management and organizational skills
- communication and listening
- branding, marketing, and networking skills
- money management
- customer service skills
- marketing skills
- critical thinking
- analytical and problem-solving skills
- conflict resolution
- self-discipline
- resourcefulness
- technical skills
- adaptability
- emotional intelligence

If you think you lack entrepreneurial skills, don't worry, as there is always room for learning, improvement, and growth. You can go through the steps we discussed earlier for skill development.

Now, let's see how to combine skills, knowledge, and talent to generate business ideas. For example, if you are detail-oriented and have a sound understanding of bookkeeping, along with an ability to engage with people and perform technical, analytical, and problem-solving skills, you can start an online accounting service or work as a virtual assistant. Likewise, you can package all your skills, knowledge, and talents into the right side hustle option.

Once you have an idea, you need to evaluate whether there is a need for your business idea in the current market. You need to analyze and ask yourself questions such as: Are there customers for my business? Will my business provide something valuable to customers or fill a need people have? In the next chapter, we will be discussing these areas in detail. However, keep in mind that your decision to pursue entrepreneurship should always be based on a realistic assessment of your skills, knowledge, talents, and willingness to embrace the opportunities and challenges.

Evaluating the Scalability and Sustainability of Different Side Hustles

How many of you have multiple ideas for side hustles but are not sure how to choose the perfect one? This section is for you! Here, I will be discussing the most popular side hustle options, weighing their pros and cons. Based on this evaluation, you can get an idea of how to select the most feasible side hustle option. Let's begin!

- **Create a podcast:** This is one of the easiest and cheapest side hustles to launch and build. You can record your audio files using audio recording apps, then edit and upload them to podcasting platforms such as iTunes, Anchor, Buzzsprout, and more. You can earn money through sponsored content, affiliate links, and ad links in the podcast descriptions, as well as paid subscriptions.

- **Start a blog:** This side hustle is perfect for those who love writing and sharing information. First, select a specific niche such as beauty, fashion, travel, food, or anything you are interested in. Then, buy a domain and build a blog website using a content management system such as WordPress or a website builder like Wix, GoDaddy, Squarespace, and more. Next, set up and design your blog, brainstorm blog topics, and write your first blog post using the attractive blog templates and design tools that many of the above-mentioned sites offer. If you successfully attract traffic, you can monetize the blog with ads or affiliate sales.

- **Influencer marketing:** This is another side hustle that costs nothing to start. First, choose a specific niche and get to know your audience. Then, select the channels you are going to use to promote yourself, such as Instagram, Facebook, YouTube channels, affiliate websites, blogs, and podcast channels. Next, build a content strategy for planning, creating, publishing, managing, and governing content, as well as attracting and engaging a target audience. Ensure that you improve your online presence and post unique content regularly. As an influencer, you can earn money from product reviews, affiliate links, sponsored content, entertaining videos, how-to tips and tricks, and much more.

- **Become an affiliate marketer:** This is a great way to earn money through multiple types of side hustles. For instance, if you have a blog site and YouTube channel in which you post content related to cooking, you can advertise and promote kitchen equipment on your platform and get a commission from the supplier for any sale that comes from your referral. In other words, if some of your viewers or users click an affiliate link or code related to kitchen equipment, you will get a commission. ClickBank, ShareASale, and ConvertKit are the most popular affiliate marketplaces.

- **Offer digital marketing services or sell digital products:** There are millions of online businesses out there, and they require individuals who are specialized in creating content, optimizing websites, graphic designing, running social channels, and so on. If you have skills related to these areas, you can start advertising your services on gig or freelance sites or on your own social media platform or website. Creating and selling digital products is another low to no-cost side hustle idea. Digital products refer to non-physical assets that can be downloadable or stream-able files such as MP3s, PDFs, videos, and templates. Digital products could include web-based applications, software, website design templates, graphics, digital art-work, photography, logos, music, and video, among many more. You can create these digital products using photo, video, graphic, and music software or apps and sell them through your website or Etsy or creative marketplaces such as Shutterstock, Canva, iTunes, Envato Market, SoundCloud, Creative Fabrica, and many more.

- **Tutoring, online courses, or coaching programs:** If you are likely to teach, this side hustle idea is for you. If you have specialized knowledge in any subject, you can start teaching or tutoring online or in person through teach-ing platforms such as Cambly, Preply, TutorOcean, and Learn to Be. I know so many young adults have started teaching and offering exam prep services while in school. So, give it a try and see! In addition to tutoring, you can create an online course or design a coaching program and sell it through online course platforms such as Udemy, Thinkific, and Podia.

- **Virtual assistant:** If you are a tech-savvy and orga-nized individual, you can register for platforms such as TaskRabbit, ChatterBoss, and Upwork and then offer your services as a virtual assistant. In this role, you will handle tasks like appointment scheduling, data entry, travel book-ings, replying to emails, and more. You will need a reliable computer and internet connection, but other than that, there are no significant costs.

- **Tech setup services:** If you are a tech whiz, you can offer your services for setting up computers, cell phones, home networks, and smart home devices. In addition, you can also offer other handyman services like fixing a fan or light switch. You can market yourself in your community as well as via social media and handyman apps such as HelloTech, Thumbtack.com, Angi, and TaskRabbit. Startup and ongoing costs are minimal, but you might need to invest in a few tools to help with installations.

- **Self-publishing e-books:** If you have a creative story or the ability to explain how to do something, you can turn it into a book and self-publish it as an e-book on platforms such as Amazon, Barnes & Noble Press, Smashwords, Lulu, and more. However, you don't need to be a skilled wordsmith. Instead, you can hire ghostwriters and editors to complete your book. While publishing an e-book is generally low cost, prices can vary depending on the length of the book and other areas, such as cover design. Most e-book platforms are free to publish, but they will take a percentage of the sale price.

- **Become an e-commerce reseller or drop-shipping:** Compared to other side hustle ideas, getting into e-commerce reselling requires a larger initial investment and time commitment as you have to purchase inventory and market a variety of products from different suppliers. You have the option of utilizing well-known e-commerce platforms such as Shopify, WooCommerce, Wix, and Squarespace. Alternatively, you can do drop-shipping without purchasing, stocking, and shipping the items you sell. Drop-shipping can be considered as an order fulfill-ment method. You need to work as an e-commerce retailer on a platform that integrates with drop-shipping vendors such as Shopify, WordPress with WooCommerce, and BigCommerce. Then, you need to promote products and provide an online storefront. Once a customer places an order, you send the order to the drop-shipping suppliers, including AliExpress, Doba, and Sprocket, who then ship the order to the customer.

- **Create and sell your own handmade goods:** If you are skilled at crafting, knitting, painting, jewelry making, or carpentry, you can create crafts and sell them online or at local markets and festivals.

- **Participate in paid online surveys:** Many companies and market researchers want to know what people think of their products and services, and they use surveys to do that. So, you have the option to participate in online surveys on survey platforms like Survey Junkie, Branded Surveys, and Swagbucks. By taking part in surveys, you can accumulate points that can be exchanged for cash, gift cards, or contributions to charitable organizations at a later time. Filling out the survey won't give you a huge amount of cash, but it will give you some pocket money for the weekend.

- **Get paid to test apps and websites:** This is quite similar to the previous side hustle idea. Many companies want to get feedback from users regarding their websites and apps before they go live. You can take usability tests through user testing platforms such as UserTesting, Enroll, UTest, UserCrowd, and Userlytics. As a tester, you are required to go in and push all the links and play with all the buttons to make sure things work properly. Once the test is approved, you'll get paid. Some competitive user testing platforms offer $100 for a 60-minute test (Ferguson, 2023).

In addition to the above side hustle ideas, here is a list of other ideas that you may consider.

- sell your photography
- sell artisan products
- sell print-on-demand (pod) products
- sell products using retail arbitrage
- sell proprietary goods
- sell private label products
- deliver packages, groceries, and other items
- become a rideshare driver
- rent out your home or a spare room
- personal assistant
- senior sitting and companion
- babysitting and childcare
- offer pet sitting, dog walking services, or doggie daycare
- offer services like car washing and detailing
- mow lawns and do other landscaping tasks
- give tours of your neighborhood

I hope you can find a side hustle opportunity from the list above that matches your personal interests, skills, knowledge, and talents. However, some opportunities may seem like great money-making side hustles at first, but they might require a lot of effort, time, and money and provide you with limited returns. So, here is a list of red flags to watch out for when considering a side hustle.

Certain side hustles, such as salons, real estate, accounting, and tax preparation services, require specific education and licensing or certification. Completing your initial education and paying initial and annual licensing fees could be costly. Similarly, you may have to put in a lot of effort and time, but there is no guarantee that you'll be able to make enough extra cash to cover the high costs. Therefore, the above-mentioned fields are very suitable if you're hoping to build a career.

Another opportunity you have to be careful of is Multilevel Marketing (MLM) Schemes, which require hefty costs and product investment, as well as time and effort. The majority of MLM companies are good at convincing people of easy money and big profit potential. However, in most scenarios, you are supposed to build a large team of downstream salespeople. I'm not saying every MLM scheme is not good. If you're capable of high-pressure sales, MLM will work for you, but if you can't manage the high workload, you might end up with a stack of unsold items and no profits.

Recently, side hustle coaching programs have been popping up, promising individuals quick success, and many marketers will convince their followers to pay hundreds or thousands of dollars for their "foolproof" system. Before registering for these programs, check whether they offer sound techniques and good advice. Nonetheless, there are plenty of free resources such as Google articles, YouTube videos, and e-books that will help you launch and grow your side hustle. Here is a list of resources that will help you find side hustle ideas and opportunities:

- The SideHustleSchool.com podcast

- SCORE.org

- Side Hustle Nation podcast and blog

- Side Hustle Pro podcast

- The Side Hustle Show podcast

- Ryan Robinson's podcast and blog

- Side Hustle Websites
  - Fiverr
  - Upwork
  - Care.com
  - Mercari
  - Rover
  - Urbansitter
  - Nextdoor
  - Steady
  - SolidGigs

Before we move on to the next chapter, it is best if you refer to the StrengthsFinder 2.0 by Gallup book to discover your strengths and learn how to use your greatest natural talents to get the most out of your life.

A Beautiful Location: 30°31'26.6"N 87°54'43.8"W

READY TO MAKE YOUR BEST DECISION YET?

Download your FREE Pro/Con Analysis Worksheet now and start making choices with confidence.

What's Inside?

- **Time Management:** Evaluate how your decision will impact your time.

- **Financial Considerations:** Understand the monetary implications before you decide.

- **Skills & Resources:** Identify what you have and what you'll need to succeed.

Why Use This Worksheet?

- **Structured Approach:** Our prompts guide you through every aspect of your decision.

- **Clarity & Confidence:** Gain a clearer understanding of the potential outcomes.

- **Informed Decisions:** Avoid regret by making a choice that aligns with your goals and values.

Stuck on a Big Decision? Get Clarity with Our Free Pro/Con Analysis Worksheet!

Making a tough decision? Whether it's a new business venture, a career move, or a personal choice, the stakes are high—and so is the stress. What if you had a simple tool to help you weigh the pros and cons, consider all angles, and make a confident decision?

FIREWATCH BUSINESS
Your Partner from Progress to Accomplishment

CHAPTER 3

Market Research and Trend Analysis

Currently, I believe that each one of you might have at least one idea for a side hustle. However, it's not always feasible to start it at once, as it's crucial to analyze whether there is a market for your potential side hustle. To do this, we need to conduct market research. In this chapter, we will first discuss what market research and trend analysis entails. Then, we'll explore current market trends and demands. After that, I'll guide you in identifying your target audience, competition, and pricing. Finally, we'll determine what products or services you can offer to your potential customers. So, let's begin with an overview of market research.

STEP-BY-STEP GUIDANCE FOR A SUCCESSFUL MARKET RESEARCH

It's important to ensure that your side hustle idea is worth pursuing before investing a lot of time, money, and effort. Therefore, conducting market research is crucial to learn important information about your target market and potential customers to convert them into buyers. In this regard, I've outlined five essential steps for conducting effective market research.

Step 1: Determine if There Is a Market for Your Potential Side Hustle

Market research involves gaining insight into various aspects, including target industry, market, and customers, to determine whether a new product or service will be successful. Successful market research will help answer the following questions:

- **User behavior:** Who are your potential customers, and why are they interested in buying your product or service? What motivates them to take action?

- **Demand:** Does your product or service offer solutions to customers' pain points? Can you align your product to suit the demand? Is there a need for your product or service?

- **Market saturation:** This is a situation that can occur when a market no longer shows new demand for a particular product or service due to competition or the firm's offerings are less in demand. How many similar options are already available to consumers? Who are the competitors doing well in the market? Are there any unaddressed or underserved customer needs that can be turned into selling opportunities? What are the challenges of competitors? What can you do differently to fill in these gaps?

- **Market size:** This is the total number of potential buyers of a specific product or service within a certain market and the total revenue these sales could bring in. How many potential buyers exist for your product or service in the specific market, and what is the total revenue that these sales could generate? Based on this, you can predict how many people would be interested in your product or service.

- **Economic indicators:** What are the recent industry and small business trends in your target market? What is the income range of your target audience? What is their employment rate?

- **Location:** Where do your potential customers live and hang out, both geographically and online? Where and what would be the ideal way to reach them?

- **Pricing:** What do potential customers pay to your competitors? What are the attitudes about pricing for a particular product or service?

By answering these questions, you can create a bigger picture, identify niches and gaps in the market, make informed business decisions, and have a better engagement with your target audience. Additionally, one of the best places to start your market research is the local chamber of commerce, which has data available at its office that will help with the market as well as demographics. Moreover, attending the local trade or business shows and job fairs at any employer or organization is a great way to see demand in the market and the services that are in demand.

Ultimately, you'll be able to create a product or service that aligns with your audience's needs, resulting in better conversion rates, higher sales and revenue, increased customer loyalty, and better user experience.

Primary and secondary are the main types of market research methods. Primary research collects data directly from the sources, while secondary research collects data from existing third-party sources. Both types of market research use qualitative and quantitative data. Quantitative data are associated with numbers and look for relevant trends, while qualitative research is associated with words and public opinions collected from first-hand observations.

Market research can take many forms, such as interviews, focus groups, competitive analysis, pricing research, buyer persona research, brand awareness research, and more. Market trend analysis is a crucial procedure utilized by business experts, business owners, and investors to recognize and evaluate market trends using past data, allowing them to make well-informed strategic choices. Trend analysis can help you spot emerging trends early, improve forecasting accuracy, and create new products and services to meet future demand before your competitors do.

Additionally, trend analysis can help you figure out whether demand is increasing, decreasing, or remaining consistent. This information can help you become aware of the risks associated with each business or investment decision. Like market research, conducting trend analysis can give you a competitive advantage.

Let's look at some recent statistics to see what we can learn. The most popular online side hustles include freelance work, blogging, selling items, affiliate marketing, and online surveys. Around 56% of the current freelance market is in the transportation sector, and Uber and delivery driving remain prominent. Notably, 65% of side hustlers are leveraging automation to streamline their businesses, and there is a marked rise in online platforms for side hustles (40% in 2021 compared to 15% in 2015) (Side Hustle Statistics, 2024). After referring to these statistics, what are the key findings that you can observe? It is evident that the majority of side hustles use technology for their business activities, so incorporating technology is necessary to remain competitive. Here, we discuss only a few basic statistics, but by conducting proper market research and trend analysis, you can collect specific information that would be useful for your side hustle.

Step 2: Figure Out Who Your Target Audience Is

One of the most crucial elements of any business or side hustle is identifying its target audience, as they are the ones who control the market and determine how well your brand performs. Is your target audience too narrow or generic? Is it too broad? Likewise, it is essential to analyze your target audience to create products and services that people actually want to buy. By identifying who your customers are and what they need, you can easily stay ahead of the competition and save money on marketing. So, here are a few steps to identify your target audience.

Imagine yourself as the customer.

This is something I've tried personally. First of all, we have to think about whether we would buy the product or service. Are there enough features and special qualities that would encourage you to purchase? Does it provide a solution to one of your problems? If you itself answer no to these questions, do you think there will be potential customers outside? So, if you are not satisfied with your own product, there is a high chance of your product flopping. So, I think it would be best not to move forward and go back and brainstorm another idea that will actually bring you results.

Gauge the interest of your local community.

The purpose of this step is to find people in your area who could benefit from your product or service, whether in person or virtually. For example, if you are making handmade jewelry, sell it at a local craft fair and see whether you can actually generate sales. Also, this is a very good opportunity for you to engage with your shoppers directly. You can interview a few customers and try to get their honest feedback on your product. Also, you can distribute a small questionnaire to check how customers feel about your product.

When it comes to online platforms, you can sign up for local Facebook groups and promote your products. Here also, you can share an online survey and use tools like stories, and polls to get prompt feedback from the audience. These steps are a ground and feasible approach where you can test the market without risking everything and create products and services that truly resonate with your target audience.

Use Google Analytics and other social media analytics to learn more about your customers.

These are some of the best technological tools that you can have deeper insights into your potential customers. Many analytical tools provide a lot of information about website and app visitors, including demographic factors like age, gender, and income levels, as well as psychographic factors like personality traits, interests, and behaviors.

Define your buyer persona.

Buyer persona is also known as customer persona, audience persona, or marketing persona, which is a fictional representation of your ideal customer. This will help you to effectively reach prospective customers, personalize your marketing, increase customer satisfaction, and optimize communication or content strategies. Here are key characteristics you can include in your buyer persona:

- age
- gender
- location
- family size
- job titles
- income
- education level
- hobbies
- interests (what books are they reading, who are they listening too?)
- values (that your product or service would help them to achieve the goals)
- goals
- pain points
- challenges
- purchasing behavior

To create an effective buyer persona, follow these simple steps:

- **First step:** Conduct market research to gather specific and up-to-date information about your target audience.

- **Second step:** Analyze the data collected in the first step to identify patterns and trends among your customers.

- **Third step:** Based on the first and second steps, identify the common characteristics of your ideal customer.

- **Fourth step:** Create your buyer persona by giving each persona a name. You can use pre-made templates from online sources, or you can create customized ones on your own. Are you wondering how many buyer personas you should aim to create? Actually, there is no correct answer. However, it's recommended to create at least two to five personas to target multiple segments of your audience.

- **Fifth step:** If you have many colleagues or departments, such as the sales and marketing department, product development, and customer service, ensure to share your buyer persona with everyone.

- **Sixth step:** Make sure to regularly review and update your buyer persona to ensure that you retain accurate and effective data.

- **Seventh step:** Test, refine, and adjust your buyer personas over time to better reflect your target audience.

Creating buyer personas is an effective way of understanding your target customers in-depth. By doing so, you can ensure that everyone who works with your side hustle knows how to effectively target, support, and engage with your customers.

Segment your audience.

Instead of treating all of your customers in the same manner, it's better to segment your audience into different groups based on different factors such as shopper demographics, psychographic factors, buying history, or any other data point. With this information, you can develop specific strategies for each segment.

While these are some basic steps for identifying your target audience, it's important to remember that customer expectations change over time. Therefore, it's crucial to identify your target audience and reassess it annually or when there are major industry shifts. Continuously allocate resources to nurturing your customer base to sustain the ongoing growth and success of your business.

Step 3: Research Your Competition

Before you officially launch your side hustle, it's better to find side hustles or companies that are already doing what you want to do. Wait! If you feel there is high competition out there, would you give up on starting a side hustle? Keep in mind that competitors are inevitable, so you cannot avoid the competition, but you can overcome it.

Therefore, competitor research helps you understand your competitors' strengths and weaknesses, plus their business strategies, including marketing, pricing, content, and more. Studying your competition can help you prepare ahead of time for what to expect and what kind of threat competitors pose to your side hustle. Here are some tips for conducting successful competitor research:

- Determine your physical and digital competitors.

- Review competitor products and see if their existing products are helping customers.

- Analyze the competitor's sales funnel, which shows all the stages customers go through before buying, to understand your competitor's sales and marketing methods.

- Track your competitor's social media strategies, content style, content type, and posting times to figure out how to stand out your brand on social media. This method will also help you identify the right social media platforms for targeting and the right content for your audience.

- Analyze your competitors' pricing and other perks they offer.

- Evaluate what technology your competitors use.

After collecting this data, it's better to perform a SWOT analysis to summarize your competitor's strengths, weaknesses, opportunities, and threats under multiple categories, including sales, marketing, products, social media, technology, shipping, and so on. Here are some questions to get you started:

Strengths Questions

- What is your competitor doing well?
- What positive attributes are associated with their brand?
- What do people know they are for?
- What is their financial situation?
- What are their employee's key strengths?
- What technologies or intellectual property do they own?

Weaknesses Questions

- What are the weaknesses of your competitor?
- What do they do poorly or inefficiently?
- What do they struggle with as a company?
- Where are they wasting money?
- Are there any negative attributes associated with their brand?
- What customer complaints or issues persist?
- What outdated technologies or processes are they using?

Opportunities Questions

- Are there opportunities in the market that your competitor has identified?
- What emerging market trends or changes can they take advantage of?
- Are there unexplored niches or segments in the market?
- What resources do they have that are currently underutilized?
- What emerging technologies can benefit them?
- Can they expand their product or service offerings?

Threats Questions

- What market trends or changes pose a threat to them?
- Are there new competitors entering the market?
- What disruptive technologies and changes in regulations or policies might challenge them?
- Are there shifts in customer preferences or economic downturns?
- Are there potential legal or litigation threats?
- Are there environmental or sustainability threats?

Once you completed the SWOT analysis for your competitors, conduct a separate analysis for your side hustle as well. After that, compare their weaknesses against your strengths and vice versa. By doing this, you will uncover areas for improvement within your own side hustle while answering the following questions: What are your competitive advantages and key strengths? Are there new product verticals you should test? Are there underserved customer needs you can address? Are there new geographic markets you can enter? Are there untapped distribution channels you could pursue? Can you introduce new marketing or sales strategies? What experiments should you try to validate opportunities? What resources do you lack? We will use the information collected from market and competitor research for our next two sections, where we determine which products to offer and under which price ranges.

Step 4: Decide What Products and Services You Will Offer and Pricing

Based on the information you gathered in the previous steps and considering your preferences, think about what kind of product or service you could offer. Next, produce a minimum viable product (MVP). This is a product with sufficient features to attract early customers who can offer feedback and confirm your product idea early in the product development process. The primary goal of creating an MVP is to evaluate your side hustle product or service idea with actual users before investing a substantial budget in the full development of the product. MVP will help you understand what resonates with your target market and what doesn't. Based on this information, you'll be able to develop your product with the right features, potentially avoiding unnecessary work and releasing your product to the market as quickly as possible.

Now it's time to set the prices for your products and services. This is one of the most challenging parts of starting a side hustle because, at the same time, you need to be competitive as well as profitable in the long term. Some people establish prices while only considering their costs, but it's essential to take into account your competitors' prices as well. That's why I included checking the pricing factor under competitor analysis as well. Here are some questions that will help you figure out your product's prices:

- What are the direct costs of your product or service?
- What are your business's indirect expenses?
- What is your breakeven point (the point where the total cost and total revenue are equal)?

- What are your competitors' prices and their offerings?
- What is the current state of your industry and the overall economy?

Once you clarify these areas, estimate the customer values you bring to your customer. Customer values refer to the unique qualities that customers value in a business's products or services.

Customer values can be categorized into four main sections: functional, emotional, life-changing, and social impact. The functional values primarily center on a product or service's attributes and its ability to meet the practical requirements of customers. In contrast, emotional value pertains to the positive emotions that customers experience from the products and services provided by a business. Life-changing customer values are linked to a customer's self-perception and desire to express themselves, while social-impact customer values occur when a customer's purchase positively impacts the lives of others.

If you're wondering how you can deliver these values to your customers, here are some examples. When it comes to your functional values, you can think of how convenient or affordable a product is. Some customers get a feeling of being on-trend or early adopters when they buy the latest technological gadgets, while others may feel a sense of luxury and exclusivity when they carry the latest designer handbag. All these feelings fall into life-changing values. Some customers are highly satisfied when they get opportunities to donate to charity as part of their purchase, and this falls under social impact values.

Developing your products or services in a way that engages with customers according to their values can increase customer loyalty to your brand. Let's see how you can consider customer values in pricing factors. If you think you're offering less value to your customers, it's better to charge a lower price than your competitors. In contrast, you can charge a higher price when you offer more value compared to your competitors. Before you officially set the price, you can contact some customers and test whether they are willing to pay for the products or services and for the outcome and value they'd be getting. If not, you have to turn back and set a newer price so that you can reach more customers.

Last but not least, ensure your pricing has a profit margin which is sales revenue that you can keep as a profit, after subtracting all costs. In reality, there is no point in running a side hustle if you cannot generate profits. Some entrepreneurs target only for a daily cash flow but profits are essential to build and scale your side hustle.

In addition to these steps, I would highly recommend you determine whether your side hustle offers more than just monetary value to your life. Rather than focusing on a "get rich quick" business idea, look for a side hustle that improves you as a person. Understand how your side hustle offers equal value to both customers and workers. Think about whether your product or service can make the world a better place, even in a small way, as nowadays, customers and investors are more likely to engage with businesses that consider the social impact and ethical side. Alright, it's time to move on to Chapter 4! where we'll explore the time allocation for your side hustle.

CHAPTER 4

Assessing Time Commitment

To determine the feasibility of a potential side hustle, analyze the amount of time you are willing to devote to it. While the side hustle may seem fun at first, failing to follow your plan can lead to failure. To be successful, you must adhere to your plan and reevaluate as you go. Therefore, it is better to analyze whether you want to do this side hustle in your free time. Can you see yourself doing this for years to come? Can it turn into a full-time gig at some point? Are you willing to skip a party or family gathering to have a meeting with your suppliers? If the answer is no, your side hustle will likely languish and fail, whereas if the answer is yes, then the side hustle may be worth pursuing. In this chapter, we discuss how to manage your time effectively and the methods of increasing productivity.

How to Effectively Juggle a Side Hustle With Other Commitments

Initially, running a side hustle can be overwhelming, confusing, and draining, making it difficult to get things done on time. It may take some time to discipline yourself to effectively manage your time and get all your work done while juggling a full-time job, family commitments, and a side hustle. However, some individuals fail to manage all these areas successfully. They usually experience burnout, stress, frustration, and other negative emotions regarding their work. As a result, they feel tense, irritable, and a little more tired or have trouble focusing. Without proper self-attention, though, these issues could worsen. However, with effective time management, prioritization, and a healthy work-life balance, you will be able to manage any of the negative emotions and have a proper balance between your side hustle and all your other responsibilities. Here is a list of tips to help you achieve these tasks:

- **Establish clear goals:** What do you want to achieve with your side hustle? Do you want to make extra income or eventually make it your main source of income? Understand your objectives, prioritize tasks, and manage your time accordingly. For example, if you want to turn your side hustle into your main source of income, you need to work hard and allocate more time to make it succeed.

- **Be organized and plan:** Sometimes running a side hustle requires you to have a clear idea of the multiple workflows. Being organized and working according to plan are some of the best things you can do to effectively manage your workflow, time, and energy. This strategy will help you make decisions more quickly without any unnecessary delays. Keep your plans simple and break down any big task into small actionable steps.

- **Prioritize and schedule:** Time is your most precious resource, and while you can't manage time, you can manage your priorities. If you are juggling a full-time job, family, and a side hustle, focus on one at a time because multitasking is the most unproductive way to fulfill tasks. Create a weekly schedule, prioritize tasks based on urgency and importance, and dedicate separate time blocks. When you are at home, focus on your family, when you are at the office, focus on your job, and when you're doing your side hustle, focus on that. Don't forget to stick to this schedule and stay consistent. Here, you can follow another method called batch task, where you complete similar tasks in one time block.

- **Create a routine and track your time:** First, jot down everything you need to do and then decide the time at which you'll complete those tasks. For instance, dedicating your morning hours to creating business strategies and having meetings with stakeholders in the afternoon. This way, everyone involved knows what needs to be done on specific days and times and can adjust their schedules accordingly. Setting reminders is another powerful method of triggering yourself to complete tasks, and it also helps you to remember important tasks, as well as keep you on track and focused. Remember to schedule breaks into your daily routine to recharge and work more efficiently. Track your time and the tasks you accomplish to ensure they align with your goals. For example, if you are spending the majority of your afternoon hours on too many meetings and you don't see the return on that investment, you know that some adjustments need to be made.

- **Set realistic expectations for time management and use time management tools:** There is no point in allocating plenty of tasks, knowing that you couldn't fulfill everything within that given period. When you fail to achieve all the tasks, you might end up with anxiety or stress, which can even ruin your overall productivity. So, always be realistic! To boost your efficiency, leverage technology and automate your tasks. You can get the help of time management tools such as to-do lists, calendar apps, and project management apps. Additionally, you can use certain time management techniques. There is no one-size-fits-all approach to the way you manage time, and you must find the best way for you. I will say that if one method is not working, drop it and move on to the next method. Find one that works—that will increase your chances of success.

- **Get comfortable with the word "no" and respect your boundaries:** Sometimes it could be difficult for you to say "no," but it's essential. For example, once, my manager asked me to train a junior employee during office hours. At first, I considered it a great opportunity, but later, I felt it negatively affected my performance at work as well as my side hustle. When I allocated more time to mentor the new employee, I didn't have enough time to complete my daily tasks at the office, and I had to bring them home and finish. In other aspects, I had to compromise the time I allocated for my side hustle. So, it's better to be aware of how much time you can spare on an additional task or responsibility. If you don't have that knowledge or confidence, don't take it on. Also, set boundaries for yourself and stick to them, and this is especially applicable for remote workers. Certain remote workers work until midnight. If they could fix a boundary that their workday ends no later than 6 p.m., they can allocate the rest of their day to spend with family or for their side hustle. To achieve this task, follow a shutdown routine at the end of your working day. Start by reviewing your calendar and listing tomorrow's tasks. Check whether there are any meetings and prioritize your top 3 tasks to work on the next day. Shut down your computer, log off from other working tools or apps, plug your phone in to charge, and walk away from them until the next morning. This shutdown routine allows you more mental space and helps you to focus on time with your partner, family, and friends.

- **Use some of your peak productivity time:** If you think that you are more productive in the morning hours then it would be best for you to spend a few more morning hours on your side hustle. However, if you are working a full-time job from 9 to 5, then why not arrive at work an hour early and work on your side hustle from 8–9 a.m.?

- **Minimize time-wasting activities and eliminate distractions:** Whether you are at home, doing your side hustle, or in the office, countless things can steal your attention away from what you are doing. Unnecessary meetings, emails, personal conversations with co-workers, social media disorganization, and procrastination are the most common time-wasting activities and distractions many of you encounter, So be mindful of them and try to avoid them as much as you can. Always create a designated workspace with the necessary tools in a quiet area. During work hours, let others know you will be unavailable.

- **Practice mindfulness:** This is an excellent way to manage stress and reduce anxiety and depression. Take a few minutes of your day to practice mindfulness techniques such as deep breathing, mindful eating, meditation, yoga, gratitude list, and so on.

- **Look for crossover opportunities:** Check whether there are any serendipitous moments where the work you're doing at your full-time job can also help with your side hustle. For example, imagine you are working as a human resources assistant manager, and you get an opportunity to participate in a training session that discusses new digital tools, including digital marketing. If you are running a side hustle that offers virtual assistance support, you can use those digital marketing tools to promote your tools.

Isn't it amazing? So, if you could find skills and activities that can serve both your side hustle and your full-time job, practice them and try to improve them more.

- **Outsourcing and delegating as much of your life and work as possible:** There is no rule that you have to manage everything when you are doing a side hustle. It's totally fine to seek support in areas that you can't manage alone. If you think you can delegate certain tasks (e.g., transporting raw materials) to your family members, friends, or others who support your side hustle, please do it. You can outsource certain tasks to suitable service providers, such as managing finance. These methods will help you manage heavy workloads, allow you more time to focus on the most important tasks, improve efficiency and flexibility, and reduce costs.

In addition to these steps, it's wise to include your family and leverage the strengths and emotional support they have in making the side hustle successful, from visioning, planning, marketing, product development, and so on. I know a person who conducts baking classes, and her younger sister helps her conduct classes while the eldest one takes care of all digital marketing and promoting classes. So, your family would be your first and biggest supporter. Once you follow these steps, trust me, you can become an expert juggler.

ENJOY!

CHAPTER 5

Financial Considerations

Natasha Munson, a motivational speaker, once said, "Money, like emotions, is something you must control to keep your life on the right track" (Slifka, 2019). This quote suggests that just like you need to keep your emotions in check, it's equally important to manage your finances effectively. Proper financial management is crucial when starting a side hustle. Therefore, in this chapter, we will discuss how to set financial goals, methods of funding your side hustle, and tips for managing your money. Let's start by discussing financial goals.

SETTING FINANCIAL GOALS FOR THE SIDE HUSTLE

A financial goal refers to monetary targets you plan to achieve. Short-term, mid-term, and long-term goals are the main types of financial goals. Short-term goals can be achieved within one year, and building an emergency fund is an example. Achieving a mid-term goal usually takes one to five years, and saving for the down payment of a car or a new house are examples. Long-term goals, like saving for retirement, usually take more than five years.

When it comes to side hustles, you can have financial goals like purchasing new machines, expanding to new markets, and so on. To give you a clear idea, let's consider starting a side hustle as a financial goal. Here are the steps you can follow when setting any type of financial goals:

- **Make your goal specific and measurable:** Once you have decided on the correct side hustle for you, set what you want to start and set an exact amount that you can measure to know if you have achieved your goal or not. To do this, you need to consider the monetary factor of your goal and create a startup budget that covers expected business costs as well as business revenue. This will help you determine how much money you need to make it through the first few months and what expenses you need to cover. Startup costs can be classified into two categories: startup assets and expenses. Startup assets are one-time purchases that you'll need to make, such as inventory, property, machines, and security deposits. Startup expenses, on the other hand, are fixed or variable costs that you'll need to pay before opening your business. Rent is an example of a fixed startup cost. Then, determine your fixed costs, also known as overhead costs. These are the costs that you'll need to bear regardless of how much you sell or produce. Examples of fixed costs include rent, business insurance, internet, and phone services. You should also estimate your variable costs, which can vary depending on your sales and production. Examples of variable costs include raw materials, utilities, shipping costs, transportation, marketing, and advertising costs. Once you've determined your costs, you should forecast your potential revenue and funding sources. This can include product or service sales, savings, interest income, or loans. You should calculate how much money you can cover from your funding sources and how much you'll need to find. By doing this, you'll be able to get a clearer understanding of your financial situation and make informed business decisions. You may use the following simple startup budgeting template published by Google Sheets: <u>Simple Startup Budgeting Template</u>.

- **Set a deadline:** Once you have your budget in place, set a deadline for when you want to achieve your goal. Make sure to set a reasonable timeline that is also a little challenging to keep you motivated. For example, I will start my side hustle in the clothing industry on a certain date. Make it specific.

- **Set goals that make sense for you:** Don't feel pressured to pursue the same goals as your friends or family members. In other words, just because all your friends are starting freelancing businesses doesn't mean you need to do the same thing. Let your own dreams shine!

In addition to these key steps, to stay on track and motivated, write your goals down and keep them where you can see them daily, and review progress daily. Eventually, you will be able to move it to weekly in time. You can also find an accountability buddy to cheer you on and check in as you work toward your goal. This person can be a family member, friend, or someone who can truly be a cheerleader. Remember, you can set goals for any target you want to achieve on your side hustle. Just follow the steps we've discussed above.

How to Fund Your Startups?

Starting a side hustle can be challenging, especially when it comes to finding the necessary funding. Even with a great business idea, you still need money. Based on the budget we created earlier, you should have an idea of how much you currently have and how much you need to start your side hustle. With this in mind, you can consider the following startup funding options. It's important to choose a funding option that aligns with your company's goals.

Self-Funding

I recommend this option to anyone starting their own business. Studies show that 39% of business founders use personal funds to finance their startups (Kirsch, 2023). So why not you? Self-funding should be your first resort, and all the other options come next. If you don't have sufficient savings to put toward your business immediately, consider free or inexpensive resources to get started.

Bartering is a great option for financing big purchases, such as furniture, without using cash. You can exchange goods or services with another party that has a mutual understanding. Another option for self-funding is bootstrapping, where you use early startup revenue to continue running the side hustle instead of seeking outside funding like loans or investors. Alternatively, you can create a small sample set of products instead of a full-blown product line and promote them through social media and other blog platforms. Then, you can rely on early customers who believe in your business idea, and their payments alone can fund the startup in the beginning. While these methods may result in slower growth, they come with less risk.

Family and Friends

While some people advise keeping friends and family separate from your business, your family and friends can be valuable resources when it comes to funding. Your closest ones are the ones you can trust the most, and they might agree to work with you without immediate payment. However, borrowing money from family can sometimes be challenging, so be careful not to damage your relationships. So, it's better to have a rough business agreement with them and ensure that you discuss and clarify all the terms beforehand.

Angel Investors

Angel investors, private investors, or silent partners are high-net-worth individuals who are likely to invest in other businesses for equity or partial ownership. However, the majority of angel investors prefer to invest in established companies rather than startups. Therefore, it's important to research the right angel investor and present your side hustle idea in a way that makes them feel invested. You can meet potential angel investors by attending industry events, conferences, forums, angel investor networks, and angel groups. In your proposal, clearly indicate your financial situation and provide realistic financial projections for your side hustle to demonstrate how much funding you need to execute your side hustle idea. Additionally, include a brief section that highlights your founding team and develop a short presentation that you can use to pitch to busy investors.

Bank Loans

Obtaining a personal or small business loan can be a great option for individuals with a high credit score. For your further information, a credit score is a three-digit number that reflects a borrower's creditworthiness. A higher credit score makes it more likely for lenders to offer loans with lower interest rates and quicker approval times. The funds from loans can be used for various purposes, such as starting a side hustle, expanding a business, purchasing supplies and equipment, managing cash flow, or covering operating expenses. When obtaining funding through a loan, you do not need to give up a share of your side hustle in exchange for the loan, which is a huge advantage.

However, it's important to have a clear understanding of how you intend to use the loan funds. Many people who take out loans to fund their businesses end up using the funds for personal purposes, ultimately failing to fulfill the primary purpose of starting their own business. Keep in mind that loans can be expensive because they must be repaid with interest, and regular loan payments are required, regardless of the side hustle's performance. This can be challenging, especially in the early stages when revenue is often tight.

Moreover, taking out loans for your side hustle can lead to personal liability. This means that if your side hustle doesn't succeed, you could be personally responsible for repaying the loan, putting your personal finances at risk. Additionally, getting approved for a loan can be challenging because most lenders prefer to work with businesses that have a proven track record. Qualifying for a loan can be challenging and time-consuming, especially with bad credit.

Some lenders have restrictions regarding using a loan for startup funding, such as requiring collateral like your home or car to qualify for the loan. This situation also can put your assets at risk if you are unable to repay the loan. As you can see, there are both pros and cons to taking a loan to fund your side hustle. Therefore, it's important to carefully weigh these factors and shop around for the best rates and terms before choosing a specific lender.

Crowdfunding

This is a low-commitment strategy for obtaining support and growing your side hustle. Crowdfunding platforms gather small amounts of capital from a large number of individuals to fund a new business venture in exchange for a reward, such as equity (shares/ownership in your business) or the first available offering of your product or service. It's important to note that you'll need to pay fees to the crowdfunding platform when you raise money, and these fees will be based on the total amount you raise. In addition, there may be significant tax implications, and you'll need to put in extra effort to run a successful funding campaign. Most importantly, if the funding goal isn't reached, pledged financing will be returned to investors, which can harm your or your side hustle's reputation. GoFundMe, Kickstarter, and Indiegogo are the most popular crowdfunding websites, so choose the platform that best aligns with your side hustle.

Grants

A grant is a sum of money given to a business to help it start or run more efficiently. Usually, government, company, foundation, corporate, or nonprofit entities provide business grants. Typically, grants are considered gifts, so they don't need to be repaid. However, if you fail to use the funds in accordance with the terms of the grant, you may have to pay it back—possibly with interest. Therefore, before you apply for a grant, check whether your side hustle goals and values are aligned with the organization you're applying to.

Do you think the funding process will end once you are successfully able to fund your side hustle? No, it won't. You should make a repayment plan as well. Except for a few of the options we discussed above, you must repay the money you have taken. If you do not have a proper plan or if you can't make the payment, my suggestion is not to take the funding. It is better to wait some time and go for self-funding. The following section will further help you in managing finances.

Tips for Managing Finances

Managing the finances of your new business can be a little tricky and overwhelming, but it's essential to achieving your financial goals. This may include growing your side hustle, maintaining financial stability, or maximizing profits. Below are some money management strategies that will help you keep your finances in order and set yourself up for long-term success.

- **Keep your side hustle business spending separate from your personal costs:** To maintain accurate record-keeping and efficient financial management, it's crucial to clearly distinguish between your personal and side hustle finances. Start by opening a separate bank account dedicated solely to your side hustle earnings and expenses. This will help you monitor your side hustle finances more effectively and have a clear snapshot of the business's financial health. Similarly, you can obtain a business credit card to prevent accidental mingling of personal and business expenses. However, be cautious and use your business credit cards responsibly. Make sure to pay credit card bills on time and aim to pay off the balance in full each month to avoid late fees, interest charges, or penalties from the lender, as late payments can negatively affect your credit score.

- **Keep track of income and expenses:** Budgeting will help you track how much money is coming in from your side hustle and where it's going out. This will help you identify areas where you overspend and areas where you do not take maximum advantage of the cash flow available to you and plan for future expenses. Instead of manually creating your budget, consider using a budgeting app or software to make the process easier. There are also bookkeeping systems, investment tracking tools, and software that can help you manage your finances seamlessly. Start with free options and consider investing in more advanced tools later. Regularly review and update your financial records, and set aside dedicated time each week or month to ensure all financial transactions are accurately recorded.

- **Keep your finances secure:** Financial security is one of the most important areas that you must look into because, nowadays, cyber threats pose a significant risk to side hustles. Therefore, pay more attention to protecting your financial data by using strong and unique passwords, and change passwords every three months. It is better to implement two-factor authentication or multi-factor authentication, which requires additional information to perform a task. Remember to safeguard your data, computers, and networks from online threats like cyberattacks, viruses, and malware by making sure you're using the most up-to-date security software, web browsers, and operating systems. Secure your Internet connection with firewall protection and ensure it's encrypted and hidden. Make sure to back up crucial business data and information, including financial files, accounts receivable and payable files, electronic spreadsheets, and databases. Also, do not provide any of your side hustle's financial information to third parties, and be wary of suspicious emails or messages that request sensitive information about your side hustle. On the other hand, you have a huge responsibility to protect the financial details of your customers. Therefore, choose a bank provider that provides both open banking and tokenization facilities. Open banking enables the electronic, secure sharing of financial information, subject to conditions agreed upon by customers, banks, and third-party service providers through the utilization of application programming interfaces (APIs). Furthermore, tokenization substitutes sensitive data with distinct identification symbols. These services will secure your customer's data and help you build trust with potential customers.

- **Remember to pay yourself first:** Many entrepreneurs tend to reinvest most of their earnings back into the business, which is important but don't forget the main reason for starting a side hustle—to increase your personal income. Therefore, it's crucial to set a regular salary for yourself from your side hustle earnings, ideally 10-20% of your income, before allocating funds for expenses or reinvestment. This approach ensures that you directly benefit from your hard work, allows you to save more, and helps you reach your financial goals more quickly. Additionally, these savings can serve as a safety net if your side hustle doesn't work out. While the initial amount can be small, it can be increased as your side hustle grows.

- **Manage your debt wisely:** If you have taken a loan to start your business or have a credit card to manage expenses, it's important to have a plan to reduce the amount of debt you have as soon as possible. Having debt can be a stressful experience, especially at the beginning stages of your side hustle. Therefore, create a realistic repayment plan and have a clear idea of interest rates plus repayment dates. Don't worry; with some financial discipline, you will be able to get out of debt and stay out of debt. Manage your side hustle income wisely to achieve this.

- **Have an emergency fund:** Many people believe that an emergency fund is only necessary for individuals, but this is not the case. Economic uncertainties and unforeseen emergencies can affect businesses as well. Therefore, it's wise to set aside a portion of your income as a rainy-day fund to keep your side hustle afloat during tough times.

- **Familiarize yourself with tax obligations:** In traditional employment, taxes are usually automatically withheld from your salary. However, side hustle income requires proactive tax planning. Tax regulations vary from country to country and state to state, so it's best to consult a tax professional to manage your taxes and avoid financial strain.

- **Seek professional financial advice:** When you're new to side hustles, managing your finances can be overwhelming. It's advisable to seek advice from a financial advisor, certified accountant, tax consultant, or expert in side hustles or self-employment. Their insights can help you save both time and money in the long run.

These are simple steps to help you organize your side hustle's finances with confidence. However, as your side hustle grows, financial management may become more complex. Therefore, proactively plan how you are going to streamline financial processes in the future. Well, let's move to Chapter 6, where we discuss how to launch your side hustle.

Get your FREE
Side Hustle Profit Planner!

SCAN THE QR CODE

Get your free Side Hustle Profit Planner and you'll know exactly what it takes to make your side hustle profitable. This isn't just another budgeting tool. **IT'S YOUR ROADMAP TO FINANCIAL SUCCESS.**

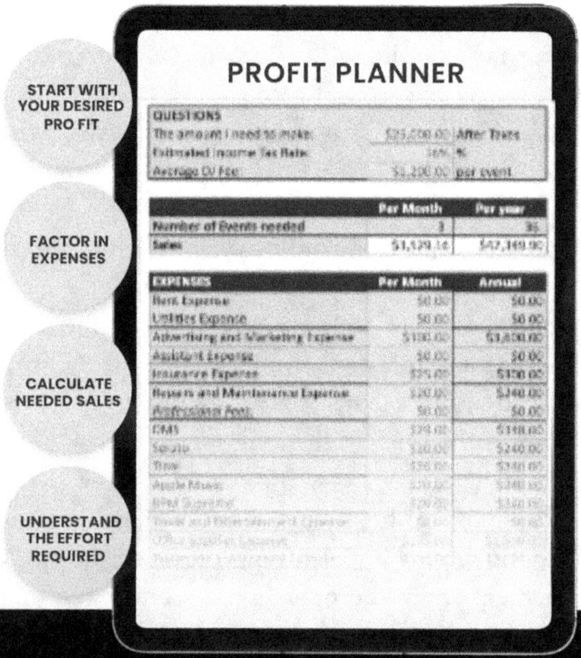

START WITH YOUR DESIRED PRO FIT

FACTOR IN EXPENSES

CALCULATE NEEDED SALES

UNDERSTAND THE EFFORT REQUIRED

PROFIT PLANNER

QUESTIONS

The amount I need to make:	$25,000.00	After Taxes
Estimated Income Tax Rate:	16%	
Average DJ Fee:	$1,200.00	per event

	Per Month	Per year
Number of Events needed	3	36
Sales	$1,129.14	$47,149.90

EXPENSES	Per Month	Annual
Rent Expense	$0.00	$0.00
Utilities Expense	$0.00	$0.00
Advertising and Marketing Expense	$150.00	$1,800.00
Assistant Expense	$0.00	$0.00
Insurance Expense	$25.00	$300.00
Repairs and Maintenance Expense	$20.00	$240.00
Professional Fees	$0.00	$0.00
DMS	$29.00	$148.00
Serato	$20.00	$240.00
Trace	$20.00	$240.00
Apple Music	$20.00	$240.00
Meal Supplies	$29.00	$349.00

CHAPTER 6

Launch Your Side Hustle

Anais Nin, the French-American diarist and essayist, once shared a powerful quote that has become an inspiration for many: "Good things happen to those who hustle" (Nin, n.d.). This quote emphasizes the importance of hard work and positioning yourself to identify opportunities to take advantage of. Starting a business venture is not easy, but I believe that with hard work and dedication, it's possible to achieve success. Therefore, now is the perfect time to put in the effort and launch your venture. This chapter offers a detailed, step-by-step guide to help you launch your side hustle successfully.

IT'S TIME TO START YOUR OWN SIDE HUSTLE!!!

Let's talk about the most exciting part of your side hustle journey: launching your side hustle! You've done a great job so far, and now it's time to shine. In this step, we'll walk you through the process of launching your side hustle successfully.

Step 1: Make a Strong Business Plan for Side Hustle

A business plan is a document that outlines your side hustle's goals and plans for achieving them. It helps your team and investors understand your vision for the side hustle and make informed decisions. Based on the information we discussed in the previous chapters, you can create a solid business plan by including the following elements:

- **Cover page:** An eye-catching cover page that includes your side hustle logo, name, address, and phone number is a great way to make a great first impression.

- **Executive summary:** This is the make-or-break section of a business plan that influences whether investors turn the page. The executive summary provides an overview of your business and highlights the most crucial pieces of your plan, such as the mission statement, side hustle's history, leadership model, overview of competitive advantages, financial projections, short-term and long-term company goals, and an ask from potential investors.

- **Company and business description:** This section provides a comprehensive overview of your company and its purpose.

- **Product and service line:** This section sets the stage for the problem you hope to solve, your solution, and how your solution fits in the market. You should include each product or service's name, its purpose, and a description of how it works. Additionally, outline your pricing model, mark-up amounts, and production costs.

- **Market analysis:** This section provides details about the target audience, the size of your total addressable market, the market's demographics, and psychographics.

- **Marketing plan:** This section emphasizes the tactical approach to reaching your target audience and provides details about advertising channels, organic marketing methods, budget, and promotional tactics.

- **Sales plan:** This section highlights how you will attract and retain customers and grow your business. Include details related to sales goals, budget, sales team structure, sales channels, sales tools, and strategies.

- **Legal notes:** This section highlights the legal structure of your side hustle and the steps you have taken or will take to operate legally, including details related to registrations, licenses, permits, and insurance.

- **Financial considerations:** This section includes your startup costs, sales forecasts for the next several months or quarters, break-even analysis, and projected profit and loss statement.

- **Appendix:** This section includes supportive materials mentioned in previous sections, such as visuals, charts, and spreadsheets.

By including these sections, you'll be well on your way to creating a strong business plan.

Step 2: Familiarize Yourself With the Law

If you are considering earning a few hundred dollars annually, you may not need to bother yourself with business entities and taxes. However, if your goal is to make a decent amount of money with your side hustle, it's important to have a bigger picture of success. Therefore, you need to determine the type of business entity that suits your needs from the following list:

- **Sole proprietorship:** This is the easiest business entity to establish because it does not require you to register your business with the state or deal with corporate formalities or paperwork requirements. As the sole owner, you are responsible for all liabilities.

- **Partnership:** This entity includes multiple owners and consists of two types of partnerships: general partnerships and limited partnerships. With a general partnership, there is no requirement to officially register the business, and all partners are directly involved in managing the business and sharing both profits and losses. On the other hand, a limited partnership is a registered business entity, and you must file paperwork with the state.

- **Limited liability company (LLC):** This entity safeguards your personal assets from the business's debts or liabilities. In other words, your personal assets are shielded. Similar to sole proprietorships and partnerships, LLCs involve minimal paperwork and ongoing requirements.

- **Corporation:** This is a good option to consider when your side hustle turns into a full-time, thriving business and you need more legal protections. Owners or shareholders do not have personal liability for the business's debts and liabilities.

It's important to note that there is no one-size-fits-all business entity type for all side hustles, as every side hustle has a unique situation. Hence, it is essential to assess the advantages and disadvantages of each type of business structure in relation to legal protection, governmental obligations, and tax considerations. Selecting the appropriate business structure is extremely significant as it influences the public perception of your business, legal liabilities, and financial matters. In summary, sole proprietorships and general partnerships are good for the starting stages, but as your business grows and generates more income, you might consider registering as an LLC or corporation. When choosing a business entity, it's better to have a risk assessment first, then seek guidance from your lawyer, accountant, tax professional, and attorney to make more informed decisions.

Step 3: Register Your Side Hustle and Get Licenses

- **Register a business name or DBA:** Registering your business name is an important step in the business registration process. The process for registering your business name can differ based on the type of registration you choose. Two types of names can be registered: business names and trade names. A business name is a legal name that you filed with your state when establishing your LLC, corporation, or another business entity. It's important to use this name for things like hiring employees, providing services, and filing taxes. A trade name, also known as a "doing business as" (DBA) name, is the name that customers and clients know your business as. This acts as a nickname for your business. For example, Trader Joe's business name is Trader Joe's Co., but their nickname will always be Trader

Joe's. A DBA is useful for small businesses that don't wish to incorporate or form an LLC.

- **Apply for an employer identification number (EIN):** The EIN is a distinct nine-digit number that is allocated to your business entity. This number enables the Internal Revenue Service (IRS) to easily distinguish your business for tax reporting purposes. If your business has employees and functions as a corporation or partnership, you must request an EIN. However, if you are a sole proprietor without employees, you are not required to have an EIN and can utilize your Social Security number for tax purposes. An EIN is advantageous for the purposes of recruiting and compensating employees, opening bank accounts, acquiring credit, and investing excess funds. It also helps keep your personal finances separate from your business finances and protects your personal information from identity theft. Depending on the type of business you operate, you may need certain licenses and permits to run your business legally. Some of the most common licenses and permits include:

  - **A home business license.** You need to obtain this if you do any work from home.
  - **An occupational permit.** You may need a specific industry permit, depending on the nature of your business. For instance, if you're planning to sell baked goods, you may require a food processing and safety permit.

It's worth noting that the rules and regulations regarding permits and licenses may vary based on your location. Therefore, it's always a good idea to visit the U.S. Small Business Administration website to determine which permits and licenses are necessary for your business.

Step 4: Hire the Right People

Before hiring an employee, you should consider whether it is necessary. Reviewing the laws of human resources in your state is important, as the laws vary wildly from state to state. Some examples of when hiring an employee is necessary include when there are inadequate resources to fill the position, when a considerable amount of time needs to be allocated, or when tapping into a different market region. If there is a valid reason, then you may proceed with the hiring process. Additionally, think about whether you need to hire a rookie person or someone with experience. Do you have a plan for training? Do you have time to train? Outsourcing? Don't forget to consider the difference and the costs between the aforementioned options. Here are some additional tips when you are building your team.

- Create a well-defined hiring plan.

- Identify the job requirements and expectations.

- Focus on employer branding.

- Write a compelling job description.

- Promote your job description on selected job boards.

- Use the power of referrals.

- Save time on hiring with prescreening (It would be beneficial to administer a skills test and also give them specific instructions to determine their ability to follow directions if they could set a test to apply to see if they follow the directions).

- Prepare the right questions and answers that you are looking for in terms of the level of knowledge and type of person that would be a good fit.

- Look for diversity in hiring.

- Run a Google search on the employee.

- Provide a positive candidate experience.

- Stay up-to-date on the industry standards for compensation.

- Set a test-drive period for the new employee (usually a 60 to 90-day probation period; be sure that the person hired knows of the probation).

- Have a solid onboarding plan.

- Have a complete employee manual or a handbook. This is a good item to outsource to a local HR company or attorney. No need for you to reinvent the wheel.

- Maintain a repository of passive candidates.

Step 5: Apply for Business Insurance

This is a critical aspect that most side hustlers overlook. The primary objective of having insurance is to safeguard your side hustle from any financial loss or liability. Therefore, it's better to consider acquiring insurance before your side gig grows too large. Insurance helps you protect your side hustle from accidents, natural disasters, and lawsuits and aids in managing risk. Here are some of the types of small business insurance you can get for your side hustle, according to the article Does Your Side Hustle Need Small Business Insurance?, (n.d.):

- **General liability insurance:** This insurance protects your side hustle from claims of accidental injuries and property damage to others, as well as other types of claims against you, such as reputational harm.

- **Workers' compensation insurance:** This insurance protects your employees if they suffer an injury or accident while on the job.

- **Commercial property insurance:** This insurance covers any type of commercial property against such perils as fire, theft, and natural disaster.

- **Business automobile policy:** This insurance provides coverage for a side hustle's use of cars, trucks, vans, and other vehicles used in the course of its business, including collision, liability, and medical coverage as a result of an accident.

- **Cyber liability insurance:** This insurance covers your business' liability for cyber threats and data breaches involving sensitive customer information.

Based on your side hustle type, select the most appropriate insurance you need to apply for. When applying, consider recommendations from other side hustlers, seek advice from a local insurance agent, and compare policies and prices.

Step 6: Consider Setting up a **Business Credit**

Business credit is a measure of the financial strength of a company, and it evaluates how creditworthy your business is. Credit bureaus generate business credit scores that range from 0 to 100 based on business credit information such as payment habits, public records of liens, and bankruptcies. Having a positive business credit score has numerous benefits, such as getting the best interest rates from lenders and insurance companies and building relationships and terms with your suppliers. Here are some tips to build your business credit:

- **Register your business and get an EIN:** Set up your side hustle as an LLC or a corporation and apply for an EIN because sole proprietorships and partnerships, the business is the same as the owner. This helps you treat your side hustle as a separate business entity from personal credit.

- **Apply for business credit:** Get a business credit score from Dun & Bradstreet credit bureaus and apply for a DUNS number.

- **Open a business checking and savings account:** Use these accounts for day-to-day business transactions.

- **Open a business credit card:** Without an established business credit profile, you can use your personal credit score to apply for a business credit card. Using a business credit card responsibly is one of the best ways to build credit for your side hustle from scratch.

- **Pay your bills on time:** Ensure you make payments on time and in full to build a stronger business credit profile over time.

- **Maintain a less than 30% credit utilization ratio:** This is the ratio that represents the amount of your total credit that you are using expressed as a percentage.

These simple steps can help you build your business credit. It's also important to check your business credit report regularly to ensure it's fair and accurate.

Step 7: Get the Right Business Tools

Incorporating business tools can help you manage your time effectively and juggle multiple tasks at once. Here are some tools you can utilize:

- **Project management:** Trello, Teamwork, and Todoist
- **Filing and storage:** Google Drive, Microsoft OneDrive, and Dropbox
- **Communication:** Social media platforms, WhatsApp and MS Teams
- **Finances:** Goodbudget, 22seven, and Fresh Books
- **Design:** Freepik, Canva, and Pixlr
- **Learning:** Udemy, Skillshare, and Teachable
- **Payment:** PayU and iKhokha
- **Stress management:** Calm and Headspace

While launching your side hustle, it's important to be aware of common mistakes in advance to avoid or mitigate them. Here's a list of common mistakes that most beginner side hustlers tend to make:

- Not doing research beforehand
- Choosing a side hustle that you don't love
- Choosing a side hustle that requires a big financial investment
- Spending all your extra money

- Not focusing well on your main income stream
- Failing to get proper business licenses and permits
- Not keeping finances in order and not using a business bank account
- Charging too little
- Not considering taxes
- Ignoring marketing efforts
- Trying to DIY everything and overworking yourself
- Not getting healthy work-life boundaries
- Ignoring the signs of burnout
- Never starting
- Giving up early

In order to launch and grow a successful side hustle, it's important to go through each step and determine which ones are necessary for your specific situation. Let's move to the next chapter, where we discuss the importance of marketing, promoting, and networking as a side hustle.

Here is anagram…It directly ties to this chapter, good luck

Try Data Sot

CHAPTER 7

Growth and Expansion

Are you ready to take your side hustle to the next level and achieve success? However, many entrepreneurs make the mistake of focusing solely on launching their side hustle and fail to consider how to grow and expand it. While taking risks and trying new things can be daunting at times, it is essential to remain motivated. As one of the Founding Fathers of the United States, Benjamin Franklin, once said, "Without continual growth and progress, such words as improvement, achievement, and success have no meaning" (Indeed Editorial Team, 2022b). So, let's dive into the exciting world of marketing and networking and discover how they can help take your side hustle to new heights. Then, get ready to learn some valuable tips and tricks on how to grow your business and measure your success. It's time to unlock your full potential and achieve the success you deserve!

IMPORTANCE OF MARKETING AND PROMOTING A SIDE HUSTLE

Many entrepreneurs believe that having a great product or service is enough to stand out in a crowded market. However, this is not true. Without an effective marketing strategy, it is virtually impossible to grow your business without breaking through the noise of your competitors. So, how can you make your side hustle known to the public? This is where marketing plays a crucial role. It not only helps you get noticed in a competitive market but also educates people about your products or services, builds trust with your customers, and keeps them coming back for more.

Marketing can boost your sales, help you maintain connections with your customers, and provide valuable feedback on your customer base as well as products or services. By having the right marketing plan in place, you can grow your side hustle significantly in a short amount of time. Therefore, it is important to allocate a significant portion of your budget to marketing. Here are some effective marketing strategies that you can use to promote your side hustle and find new clients:

- join and get involved with your local chamber of commerce
- word of mouth
- social media marketing
- blogging
- video marketing
- podcasting
- email marketing
- family and friends
- attending industry events, conferences, local sponsorships, and community events
- joining online forums and communities
- collaborating with complementary businesses
- leveraging online job marketplaces and freelance platforms
- offering free workshops, webinars, or training sessions
- writing guest posts or articles
- craigslist and local classifieds
- using search engine optimization (SEO) for more traffic

- running targeted advertising campaigns (google ads, Bing ads, Facebook ads)
- business cards
- flyers and doorknob hangers (be aware of soliciting laws)
- offering exclusive discounts or promotions
- guerilla marketing tactics

You don't need to use all of these marketing techniques. Choose the ones that best suit your business model. However, it is essential to make marketing a priority from the start and stick to your plan. Remember that every successful solopreneur with a side hustle has faced the same challenges, but they have managed to overcome them and succeed. So can you!

Significance of Networking

Let's talk about networking! Networking refers to various forms of communication and interaction between individuals or groups. In the context of business, networking involves building and maintaining professional relationships with clients and other professionals in your industry. It also involves exchanging information, ideas, business techniques, and resources, which can help you grow and succeed in your field.

But why is networking so important? Well, by connecting with other professionals or industry experts, you can identify new sales opportunities and gain a better understanding of common strategies, best practices, and industry standards. Networking is also useful for keeping up to date with the latest news and innovations and recognizing important trends. Engaging in conversations with various people in your field can provide you with diverse viewpoints and help you discover unexpected strategies for enhancing business operations. Building relationships with leaders in your industry can greatly benefit your side hustle's expansion. By seeking their expert advice, you can gain valuable insights and develop your confidence and trust. This can motivate you to pursue more opportunities in the industry. For your additional readings, I would highly recommend the book "Infinite Giving" by Ivan Misner, Greg Davies, and Julian Lewis.

To network effectively in business, there are various options available such as attending seminars, joining networking groups, joining and attending chamber of commerce events, and creating a social media profile for business networking. When you're running a side hustle, effective networking is especially crucial. Here are some tips to help you do it right:

- Connect with the right people who can offer the specific help you need.

- Be proactive and communicate with your network regularly.

- Become a resource for others and offer assistance when appropriate.

- Attend community events, company mixers, and corporate retreats often.

- Follow up with any new contacts you make at in-person or online events to demonstrate your interest in their business and your ability to hold yourself accountable.

- Develop an elevator pitch to communicate the purpose of your networking efforts quickly, which can help you form connections more efficiently.

Remember, networking isn't just about expanding your circle—it's also a fantastic opportunity to grow your business and achieve your goals. So get out there, make some new friends, and watch your side hustle soar!

STRATEGIES FOR SCALING A SIDE HUSTLE AND EXPLORING NEW OPPORTUNITIES

Are you ready to take your side hustle to the next level? With a little bit of planning and hard work, you can turn your passion project into a thriving business. Here are some actionable steps that you can take to achieve this exciting transformation:

- **Optimize your time management:** Find ways to maximize productivity and minimize distractions, such as setting specific work hours and batching tasks. You can follow the time management techniques we discussed in Chapter 4 for better results.

- **Identify growth opportunities:** Take a close look at your target market and identify areas where you can expand your offerings or reach new customers. Also, listen to your customers and actively seek feedback to improve your products or services. Staying abreast of market trends, customer pain points, and emerging markets will help you uncover opportunities.

- **Refine your value proposition:** Your value proposition is a concise statement that highlights the benefits that customers can expect when choosing your products or services. Make sure to keep it clear and simple, avoiding any jargon or business-speak. Refining your value proposition will help you differentiate yourself from competitors and attract loyal customers.

- **Focus on customer service:** Providing impeccable customer service is the backbone of a successful small business. Satisfied customers are more likely to become loyal advocates for your brand, generate word-of-mouth referrals, and create repeat businesses. Improved customer satisfaction will help you attain a competitive advantage and enhance your side hustle reputation. Therefore, treat your customers with respect, provide prompt assistance, communicate clearly, and go the extra mile to exceed their expectations. Also, educate your team members about your side hustle and its processes, encourage them to have a positive attitude, be honest when things go wrong, and focus on customer satisfaction and a sense of care.

- **Develop written systems and processes:** Creating written systems and processes can help you delegate tasks to other team members while you focus on leading. These systems can also streamline your operations and ensure consistency in your business practices.

- **Start networking and model other successful businesses:** As we already discussed in the previous section, networking is crucial for building relationships with potential customers, partners, and mentors. Take inspiration from other successful businesses, but also add your own unique touch to stand out. Plan and think of your side hustle as a major business right from the start, which will lay a solid foundation and set you up for success.

- **Track your competitors' mistakes:** While it's tempting to look to your competitors for inspiration, it's also important to learn from their mistakes. Keep track of their struggles think about how you can avoid those mistakes and tighten your business plan to steer clear of the same pitfalls.

- **Boost your online presence:** Boosting your online presence is essential in today's digital age. Therefore, create a professional website, optimize your social media profiles, and invest in online advertising and SEO.

- **Streamline operations:** Review your business processes and identify areas that can be streamlined or automated. Based on the information you get from the previous step, implementing systems and tools to handle tasks like inventory management, invoicing, and customer service can free up time and enhance scalability and resources for more significant growth opportunities.

- **Monitor finances closely:** Keep a close eye on your finances, and track revenue, expenses, and profits meticulously to make informed decisions. Most importantly, create a budget and stick to it to avoid overspending during the scaling process.

- **Incorporate different metrics:** It is advisable to use a variety of metrics to evaluate the progress and success of your side hustle and determine its overall long-term performance. Below are some metrics that can be used:

  o **Financial metrics** include revenue, profit, and expenses.
  o **Customer metrics** help you understand your customers, and they include customer acquisition cost, which measures how much it costs to acquire each customer; customer lifetime value, which is the total revenue

generated by a customer over the entire duration of their relationship with your business; and customer churn rate, which is the rate at which customers cease their relationship with your side hustle.

- ○ **Conversion metrics** include conversion rate, which shows the percentage of people who complete a specific action; the average order value, which represents the typical amount spent per customer order; and the cart abandonment rate, which indicates the proportion of visitors who add items to their cart but fail to complete the purchase.

- ○ **Engagement metrics** include website traffic, which measures the effectiveness of your online presence and marketing efforts; time on site, which measures the effectiveness of your website's content and design; and social media engagement, which measures the level of interaction and participation of your audience with your social media content and the effectiveness of your social media marketing efforts.

- ○ **Retention metrics** consist of the repeat purchase rate, which assesses the proportion of customers who make multiple purchases from your side business; average revenue per user, which calculates the mean revenue generated per user within a designated time frame; and user retention rate, which quantifies the percentage of customers who persist in using your product or service over time.

- ○ **Operational metrics** include production efficiency, which measures the ability of your business to produce goods or deliver services quickly, accurately, and cost-effectively; fulfillment and delivery time, which measures the efficiency and effectiveness of your order fulfillment process; and inventory turnover, which measures how quickly you sell and replace your inventory over a specific period.

o **Marketing metrics** include return on advertising spend, which measures the revenue generated for every dollar spent on advertising; click-through rate, which measures the percentage of people who click on an advertisement or promotional link compared to the total number of people who view it; and email open rate, which measures the percentage of subscribers or recipients who open your emails out of the total number of emails sent.

o **Competitive metrics** include market share, which measures the percentage of total sales or customers your side hustle has compared to the total market; brand awareness, which assesses the effectiveness of your branding and marketing efforts and identifies areas for improvement; and customer satisfaction index, which measures the level of satisfaction your customers' experience.

o **Social proof metrics** include customer reviews and ratings, referral rate, and number of social media followers.

o **Personal metrics** include work-life balance, personal satisfaction, and stress levels.

Remember that growing your side hustle into a profitable business is not an easy journey. You may face setbacks and failures along the way. However, you should embrace these experiences as opportunities for learning and growth. Don't be afraid to learn from your mistakes and adapt your strategies as needed.

Building a successful business takes time, effort, and dedication. But with these steps, you can turn your side hustle into a thriving business and achieve your entrepreneurial dreams. Also, don't forget to set a date for when you will turn your side hustle into your full-time income. It might take weeks, months, or even years, but setting a date will keep you on track and help you take yourself seriously as you see that day getting closer.

Before we wrap things up, list the marketing strategies that you excel at and dive deeper into them for even greater success. Plus, identify the key metrics you can use to measure your progress and celebrate your achievements. So, let's get pumped for you starting your new side hustle. It is hard work, but worth it when you see yourself achieving your goals which will lead you to success.

Fall Destination:
33°12'29.9"N 87°33'01.4"W

CONCLUSION

In this book, we have outlined the most important steps you need to take to launch and grow your very own side hustle! Imagine having the freedom to work on something you're passionate about while earning extra income on the side. It's time to pursue your dreams and turn your side hustle into a thriving business!

To make it happen, the first step is to identify your true motivation for starting a side hustle. This is followed by identifying the skills and passions you can use in your side hustle. Market research and trend analysis will then be conducted to explore current market trends and demands. This will help you identify your target audience, competition, and pricing. Next, assess how much time you can devote to your side hustle and manage your time and other commitments.

The fifth step is to find start-up funds from appropriate methods and manage finances to get the maximum benefit from the initial capital and revenue you make from selling your products and services. The sixth step is to launch your side hustle, which involves creating a solid business plan, investigating applicable laws and regulations, registering your side hustle, building a team, applying for business insurance, setting up business credit, and incorporating the right business tools. Once you have everything in place, it's time to market your business to grab customers' attention and generate more sales. Last but not least, track the growth and performance of your side hustle.

Starting a side hustle can be a challenging task, but it's important to treat it as a job and set goals and deadlines for yourself. It may be difficult, and you may face obstacles, but persevere and don't quit. Remember, where you start is not where you end up. So, if you encounter roadblocks, change your approach. Some say to always be hustlin', which is true, but I add to always be learning. So, educate yourself, hustle in silence, dream about success, and work hard for it, but let your success make the noise!

Last but not least, I appreciate you taking the time to read this book and please don't forget to share your experience as a review.

Listen:

REVIEW THE BOOK:

APPENDIXES

Here is a list of recommended books to consider adding to your reading list.

- Infinite Giving Ivan Misner, Greg Davies, Julian Lewis
- Feel Good Productivity Ali Abdaal
- The E-Myth Revisted Michael Gerber
- Atomic Habits James Clear
- The Pep Talk Robert Shook, Kevin Elko
- The Go Getter Peter B Kyne
- Born to Win Zig Ziglar
- See you at the Top Zig Ziglar
- Over the Top Zig Ziglar
- Seven Habits of Highly Effective People Stephen Covey
- Catcher in the Rye J.D. Salinger
- Side Hustle: From Idea to Income in 27 Days Chris Guillebeau

REFERENCES

Abello, C. (2021, February 26). *17 motivating ways to improve your skills.* Inspiring Tips. https://inspiringtips.com/asia/ways-to-improve-your-skills/

Adams, R. L. (2018, January 19). *5 ways to grow your side hustle into a full-time income.* Entreprencur. https://www.entrepreneur.com/starting-a-business/5-ways-to-grow-your-side-hustle-into-a-full-time-income/307660

Agaragimova, E. (2023, May 9). *The importance of a side hustle: Why everyone should have one.* LinkedIn. https://www.linkedin.com/pulse/importance-side-hustle-why-everyone-should-have-one-elena-agaragimova/

Airbnb, Inc. (n.d.). Yahoo Finance. https://finance.yahoo.com/quote/ABNB/

All About That Money. (2023, July 7). *The benefits of having multiple streams of income.* Medium. https://medium.com/@All_About_That_Money/the-benefits-of-having-multiple-streams-of-income-ea715a9b0f13

Amaresan, S. (2023, June 13). 7 undeniable reasons customer service is important to your business. *HubSpot.* https://blog.hubspot.com/service/importance-customer-service

Anderson, A. (2024, May 21). *Side hustle smarts: 5 metrics to measure success.* SUCCESS. https://www.success.com/side-hustle-smarts-5-metrics-to-measure-success/

Barker, A. (2021, June 17). *33 side hustle quotes to get your motivation flowing.* LogicalDollar. https://logicaldollar.com/side-hustle-quotes/

Beltis, A. J. (2022, March 29). How to build a detailed business plan that stands out [free template]. *HubSpot.* https://blog.hubspot.com/marketing/business-plan-template

Bergman, S. (2019, April 24). *Six hugely successful businesses that started out as side hustles.* The Independent. https://www.independent.co.uk/life-style/side-hustles-self-employed-business-twitter-airbnb-startups-a8882996.html

Biyela, F. (2021, May 17). *8 tools to start and grow your side hustle.* IKhokha. https://www.ikhokha.com/blog/8-tools-to-start-and-grow-your-side-hustle

Brownlee, M. (2023, March 21). *Side hustle metrics: What you need to consider for side hustle success.* Klipfolio. https://www.klipfolio.com/blog/side-hustle-metrics

Carmicheal, K. (2022, October 5). How to find your target audience. *HubSpot.* https://blog.hubspot.com/marketing/target-audience

Chanay, M. W. (2022, December 15). *What you must do to grow a side hustle and turn it into your dream business.* Forbes. https://www.forbes.com/sites/forbesbusinesscouncil/2022/12/15/what-you-must-do-to-grow-a-side-hustle-and-turn-it-into-your-dream-business/?sh=3d75b2c77485

Chen, J. (2023, August 24). *Small-business grants: Everything you need to know.* Investopedia. https://www.investopedia.com/terms/g/grant.asp

Cirelly, J. (2023, July 14). *Emerging side hustle trends & statistics in 2024.* Side Hustle Science. https://sidehustlescience.org/side-hustle-trends/

Collamer, N. (2018, December 3). *12 free resources to find a job, start a side hustle or change careers.* Forbes. https://www.forbes.com/sites/nextavenue/2018/12/03/12-free-resources-to-find-a-job-start-a-side-hustle-or-change-careers/?sh=5166429039ec

Council, Y. E. (2019, July 15). *10 tips for testing to see if your side hustle idea will work.* Forbes. https://www.forbes.com/sites/theyec/2019/07/15/10-tips-for-testing-to-see-if-your-side-hustle-idea-will-work/?sh=34a9904559e5

Council, Y. E. (2020, February 20). *Five benefits of having multiple sources of income as an entrepreneur.* Forbes. https://www.forbes.com/sites/theyec/2020/02/25/five-benefits-of-having-multiple-sources-of-income-as-an-entrepreneur/?sh=33fa4dba43bb

Coursera Staff. (2023, September 28). *The importance of skill development and where to start.* Coursera. https://www.coursera.org/articles/skill-development

Craig, L. (2016, August 24). *15 free tools to take your side-hustle to the next level.* Entrepreneur. https://www.entrepreneur.com/growing-a-business/15-free-tools-to-take-your-side-hustle-to-the-next-level/280491

Cruze, R. (2022, April 25). *How to set financial goals.* Ramsey Solutions. https://www.ramseysolutions.com/personal-growth/setting-financial-goals

Cybersecurity for small businesses. (n.d.). Federal Communications Commission. https://www.fcc.gov/communications-business-opportunities/cybersecurity-small-businesses

Daniella. (2022, May 9). *How to identify your skills (& turn them into a side hustle).* I like to Dabble. https://iliketodabble.com/how-to-identify-your-skills/

Diehl, E. (2022, July 14). *11 benefits of a side hustle.* SoFi. https://www.sofi.com/learn/content/benefits-of-a-side-hustle/

Difference between talent and skill. (2023, June 26). Testbook. https://testbook.com/key-differences/difference-between-talent-and-skill

Does Your Side Hustle Need Small Business Insurance? (n.d.). *Bizee.* https://bizee.com/blog/side-hustle-small-business-insurance?redirect=fromIncfile

Etzel, N. (2021a, July 19). *9 mistakes to avoid when starting a side hustle.* Www.fool.com. https://www.fool.com/the-ascent/personal-finance/articles/9-mistakes-to-avoid-when-starting-a-side-hustle/

Etzel, N. (2021b, July 19). *11 common side hustle mistakes (and how to avoid them)*. OnDeck. https://www.ondeck.com/resources/common-side-hustle-mistakes

Expert Panel. (2021, July 29). *Nine simple, low-risk ways to test whether your side hustle is a viable business idea*. Forbes. https://www.forbes.com/sites/theyec/2021/07/29/nine-simple-low-risk-ways-to-test-whether-your-side-hustle-is-a-viable-business-idea/?sh=55e99e3f4e75

Fabregas, K. (2023, December 2). *29 side hustle ideas to make extra money in 2023* – Forbes Advisor. https://www.forbes.com/advisor/business/best-side-hustle-ideas/

Farese, D. (2023, March 29). How to do market research: A 6-step guide. *HubSpot*. https://blog.hubspot.com/marketing/market-research-buyers-journey-guide

Ferguson, E. (2023, November 30). *24 side hustles to make extra money in 2023*. Shopify. https://www.shopify.com/blog/side-hustle

Flash Credit Africa. (2023, May 29). *Benefits of having multiple streams of income*. LinkedIn. https://www.linkedin.com/pulse/benefits-having-multiple-streams-income-flash-credit-africa/

Forbes Coaches Council. (2019, December 26). *12 tips for achieving work-life balance with a side gig*. Forbes. https://www.forbes.com/sites/forbescoachescouncil/2019/12/26/12-tips-for-achieving-work-life-balance-with-a-side-gig/?sh=39d4b42a4d78

Fox, M. (2019, October 21). *Your side hustle may be at risk — here are steps you can take to protect it*. CNBC. https://www.cnbc.com/2019/10/21/how-to-protect-your-side-hustle.html

Fud, Inc. (2023, June 15). *10 powerful tools side hustlers can use to boost their earnings*. Www.linkedin.com. https://www.linkedin.com/pulse/10-powerful-tools-side-hustlers-can-use-boost-earnings-joinfud/

Gesualdi-Gilmore, L. (2023, March 9). *10 solid reasons to start a side hustle asaP*. FinanceBuzz. https://financebuzz.com/start-a-side-hustle-asap

Ghosh, K. (2021, May 28). *7 reasons why you should start a side business now.* LinkedIn. https://www.linkedin.com/pulse/7-reasons-why-you-should-start-side-business-now-karmeish-ghosh/

Hargrave, M. (2021). *Market saturation: Taking it to the max.* Investopedia. https://www.investopedia.com/terms/m/marketsaturation.asp

Hedau, S. (2022, November 28). *Importance of skill development | 13 things you must know.* Softspace Solutions. https://softspacesolutions.com/blog/importance-of-skill-development/

Herrity, J. (2021). *Entrepreneurial skills: Definition and examples.* Indeed Career Guide. https://www.indeed.com/career-advice/career-development/entrepreneurial-skills

Hicks, K. (2017, September 11). *23 resources for side hustlers.* HostGator. https://www.hostgator.com/blog/resources-side-hustle/

How to create a healthy startup budget in 6 steps. (n.d.). Brex. https://www.brex.com/journal/startup-budget

How to find angel investors for your startup (7 tactics). (n.d.). Digital Ocean. https://www.digitalocean.com/resources/article/how-to-find-angel-investors

How to promote your side hustle like a full-fledged business. (2021, May 27). *The Blog.* https://blog.coastcapitalsavings.com/side-hustle/promote-side-hustle-like-full-fledged-business/

How to start a side hustle. (2023, March 19). Time. https://time.com/personal-finance/article/start-a-side-hustle/

How to turn your skills into a profitable side business. (2020, June 3). Fiverr. https://www.fiverr.com/resources/guides/business/turn-skills-into-business

Howarth, J. (2023, February 3). *Market trend analysis: A simple step-by-step guide.* Exploding Topics. https://explodingtopics.com/blog/market-trend-analysis

Hoyt, B. (2023, July 22). *7 reasons why you absolutely need a side hustle.* Forbes. https://www.forbes.com/sites/bobby-hoyt/2023/06/22/7-reasons-why-you-absolutely-need-a-side-hustle/?sh=27f20dbf512d

Humphrey, M. (2023, July 24). *11 essential entrepreneurial skills for business success.* Flippa. https://flippa.com/blog/11-essential-entrepreneur-skills-for-business-success/

Hutchings, V. (2020, June 29). *How to conduct market research for your business idea.* Tide Business. https://www.tide.co/blog/business-tips/market-research/

Indeed Editorial Team. (2020, December 10). *The importance of networking in business (tips included).* Indeed.com. https://www.indeed.com/career-advice/career-development/networking-in-business

Indeed Editorial Team. (2022a, June 25). *10 tips to become better at reviewing and evaluating resumes.* Indeed. https://www.indeed.com/career-advice/career-development/evaluating-resumes

Indeed Editorial Team. (2022b, June 25). *88 motivational quotes on growth in business to inspire you.* Indeed. https://www.indeed.com/career-advice/career-development/quotes-on-growth-in-business

Indeed Editorial Team. (2023a, February 17). *How to create an applicant screening process.* Indeed. https://www.indeed.com/career-advice/career-development/applicant-screening-process

Indeed Editorial Team. (2023b, February 17). *How to create an applicant screening process.* Indeed Career Guide. https://www.indeed.com/career-advice/career-development/applicant-screening-process

Indeed Editorial Team. (2023c, March 11). *The 8-step career planning process.* Indeed Career Guide. https://www.indeed.com/career-advice/career-development/career-planning-process

Indeed Editorial Team. (2023d, February 4). *3 types of income: Definitions and examples.* Indeed Career Guide. https://www.indeed.com/career-advice/career-development/types-of-income

Indeed Editorial Team. (2023e, September 18). *Importance of skill development and tips for growth.* Indeed. https://in.indeed.com/career-advice/career-development/developing-skills

Innocent drinks. (2019, February 15). Wikipedia; Wikimedia Foundation. https://en.wikipedia.org/wiki/Innocent_Drinks

Inuk, D. (2023, April 7). Creating buyer personas: A key step in defining your target audience. *Poptin Blog.* https://www.poptin.com/blog/creating-buyer-personas-a-key-step-in-defining-your-target-audience/

Jay. (2023, April 4). *21 real ways to market your side hustle & grow your business.* Gig Hustlers. https://gighustlers.com/ways-to-market-your-side-hustle/

Kagan, J. (2019). *Credit score.* Investopedia. https://www.investopedia.com/terms/c/credit_score.asp

Kagan, J. (2023, September 13). *Business credit score.* Investopedia. https://www.investopedia.com/terms/b/business-credit-score.asp

Kagan, J. (2024, April 3). *Employer identification number (ein): Who needs it and how to get it.* Investopedia. https://www.investopedia.com/terms/e/employer-identification-number.asp#toc-benefits-of-an-employer-identification-number

Kirsch, K. (2023, January 24). Startup funding: What it is, how it works, & 5 tips for landing it. *HubSpot.* https://blog.hubspot.com/sales/how-startup-funding-works#types-startup-funding

Kordestani, M. (2020, October 28). *Big businesses that started as side hustles.* Entrepreneur. https://www.entrepreneur.com/starting-a-business/big-businesses-that-started-as-side-hustles/358488

Kumar, B. (2022, July 11). 12 profitable hobbies you can monetize (you probably have at least one). *Shopify.* https://www.shopify.com/blog/make-money-from-your-hobbies

Loper, N. (2023, September 24). *Register your business? 10 ways to make your side hustle feel official.* Side Hustle Nation. https://www.sidehustlenation.com/register-a-business/

Measuring success: Key metrics for your side hustle. (2023, September 15). Empowered Earnings. https://www.empoweredearningsclub.com/measuring-success-key-metrics-for-your-side-hustle-2/

Mondal, A. A. (2023, July 29). *Scaling up: Turning your side hustle into a profitable small business.* Real Wealth Business. https://realwealthbusiness.com/turning-your-side-hustle-into-a-profitable-small-business/

Money Marshmallow. (2023, May 24). *How to manage your side hustle finances effectively.* Money Marshmallow. https://moneymarshmallow.com/how-to-manage-your-side-hustle-finances/

Moreno, A. (2023, September 29). 10 tips for managing your full-time job and side hustle efficiently. *Medium.* https://blog.startupstash.com/10-tips-for-managing-your-full-time-job-and-side-hustle-efficiently-e8f7277648ae

My Balancing Act. (2023, February 19). *8 money management tips for your side hustle.* My Balancing Act. https://mybalancingact.co.uk/money-management-tips-for-your-side-hustle/

Narumanchi, S. (2017, May 4). *Best tips to juggle your side hustle and full-time job.* Crowd Work News. https://crowdworknews.com/best-tips-juggle-side-hustle-full-time-job/

Nin, A. (n.d.). *Anais Nin quotes.* Goodreads. https://www.goodreads.com/quotes/348099-good-things-happen-to-those-who-hustle

Olito, F. (2020, March 31). *13 famous companies that started out as side hustles.* Business Insider. https://www.businessinsider.com/companies-started-as-side-hustles-2019-8

100+ small business quotes for motivation & inspiration. (n.d.) *CheckMark Blog.* https://blog.checkmark.com/small-business-quotes-for-motivation/

Organ, C., & Bottorff, C. (2022, October 18). *Employee handbook best practices in 2022.* Forbes Advisor. https://www.forbes.com/advisor/business/employee-handbook/

Organ, C., & Main, K. (2024, March 1). *How to register a business name (2022 guide)* Forbes Advisor. https://www.forbes.com/advisor/business/how-register-business-name/

Panel, E. (2022, May 19). *Eight things you can do right now to grow your side hustle.* Forbes. https://www.forbes.com/sites/theyec/

2022/05/19/eight-things-you-can-do-right-now-to-grow-your-side-hustle/?sh=7a6d2d521a99

Parham, J. (2023, December 29). *31 marketable skills you can learn and develop in 2024.* Indeed. https://www.indeed.com/career-advice/career-development/marketable-skills-to-learn

Payments, T. (2023, August 14). *8 money tips for managing cash flow for your side hustle.* Trust Payments. https://www.trustpayments.com/blog/8-money-tips-for-managing-cash-flow-for-your-side-hustle/

Pofeldt, E. (2021, January 27). *The ultimate side hustle guide for 2021.* CNBC. https://www.cnbc.com/guide/side-hustles/

Prakash, P. (2020, December 16). *Types of business entities.* NerdWallet. https://www.nerdwallet.com/article/small-business/business-entity

Pratt, M. K., & Lebeaux, R. (n.d.). *What is value proposition? - definition from what is.com.* SearchCIO. https://www.techtarget.com/searchcio/definition/value-proposition-VP

The pros and cons of getting a loan for your startup. (2024, February 9). FasterCapital. https://fastercapital.com/content/The-Pros-and-Cons-of-Getting-a-Loan-for-Your-Startup.html#The-Pros-Of-Getting-A-Loan-For-Your-Startup

Rask, N. (2023, January 13). The benefits and challenges of starting a side hustle. *Medium.* https://medium.com/@nickrask/the-benefits-and-challenges-of-starting-a-side-hustle-e6dd688e4b4b

Rittenberg, J. (2021, December 2). *Trade name vs. business name: What's the difference?* Forbes Advisor. https://www.forbes.com/advisor/business/trade-name-vs-business-name/

Robinson, R. (2018, October 16). *Why we need to talk about side hustle burnout.* Forbes. https://www.forbes.com/sites/ryanrobinson/2018/10/16/side-hustle-burnout/?sh=6e59e6d7e7a6

Ruby, D. (2024, May 6). *How many people use Instagram 2024 [global data].* Demandsage. https://www.demandsage.com/instagram-|statistics/

Samuel, A. (2018, June 10). *The small business guide to hiring the best employees.* Zapier.com. https://zapier.com/blog/small-business-hiring/

Sears, A. (2018, January 3). *4 common challenges to starting a side hustle.* StartupNation. https://startupnation.com/start-your-business/common-challenges-side-hustle/

7 essential tools you'll need when setting up a side hustle business. (2020, January 27). Invoice Ninja. https://invoiceninja.com/7-essential-tools-youll-need-when-setting-up-a-side-hustle-business/

75+ swot analysis questions for facilitators. (n.d.). Parabol. Retrieved February 14, 2024, from https://www.parabol.co/resources/swot-analysis-questions/

Shaffer, C. (2023, August 8). *Which hobbies or skills can turn into a profitable side hustle?* Brand Creators. https://www.brandcreators.com/which-hobbies-or-skills-can-turn-into-a-profitable-side-hustle/

Sheehy, K. (2024, February 26). *How to build business credit in 5 steps.* NerdWallet. https://www.nerdwallet.com/article/small-business/how-to-build-business-credit-small-business-loans

Shepherd, J. (2024, April 23). 33 essential Facebook statistics you need to know in 2024. *The Social Shepherd.* https://thesocialshepherd.com/blog/facebook-statistics

Side hustle statistics, trends, and insights for 2024. (2024). Gigworker.com. https://gigworker.com/hub-resource/side-hustle-statistics/

Side-hustle challenge: 5 difficulties in balancing a job and a part-time business. (2021, May 10). Startup Sloth. https://startupsloth.com/side-hustle-challenge-5-difficulties-in-balancing-a-job-and-a-part-time-business/

Slade, S. (2018, May 23). *3 tips for balancing a side hustle with a full-time job.* CNBC. https://www.cnbc.com/2018/05/22/3-tips-for-balancing-a-side-hustle-with-a-full-time-job.html

Slifka, R. (2019, February 21). *15 quotes from our favorite money saving experts.* Banking Made Awesome. https://www.chime.com/blog/15-quotes-from-our-favorite-money-saving-experts/

Smith, T. (2023, October 6). *crowdfunding: What it is, how it works, and popular websites.* Investopedia. https://www.investopedia. com/terms/c/crowdfunding.asp#toc-the-bottom-line

Sokunbi, B. (2023, August 2). *How to start a side hustle in 10 steps.* Clever Girl Finance. https://www.clevergirlfinance.com/starting-a-side-hustle/#h-10-actionable-steps-for-starting-a-side-hustle

Strengthfy. (2023, August 4). *How to turn your hobbies into marketable talents.* Medium. https://strengthfy.medium.com/how-to-turn-your-hobbies-into-marketable-talents-8320d4c00d0c

Syndication Cloud. (2019, September 2). *7 reasons why marketing is important for any small business.* Kake. https://www.kake.com/story/40992430/7-reasons-why-marketing-is-important-for-any-small-business

Szczesny, M. (2023, September 2). *How to scale your side hustle into a thriving business.* Addicted 2 Success. https://addicted2success. com/success-advice/how-to-scale-your-side-hustle-into-a-thriving-business/

10 side hustle websites you should know about. (2024, January 8). Get-schooled.com. https://getschooled.com/article/5775-10-side-hustle-sites-you-should-know-about/

Todorov, G. (2022, September 21). *11 reasons why you need a side hustle.* StartupNation. https://startupnation.com/start-your-business/11-reasons-why-you-need-side-hustle-todorov/

Tretina, K. (2023, April 14). *How to start a side hustle (and which one to choose).* LendingTree. https://www.lendingtree.com/student/start-side-hustle/#File

Twin, A. (2023, March 17). *Value proposition: How to write it with examples.* Investopedia. https://www.investopedia.com/terms/v/valueproposition.asp

Twin, A. (2024). *Key performance indicator (kpi): Definition, types, and examples.* Investopedia. https://www.investopedia.com/terms/k/kpi.asp

Udemy. (2024, May 7. Wikipedia. https://en.wikipedia.org/wiki/Udemy

Vaughan, P. (2022, February 21). *How to create detailed buyer personas for your business.* Hubspot. https://blog.hubspot.com/marketing/buyer-persona-research

Wessel, K. (2023, January 13). *How to identify your business's target audience.* Forbes. https://www.forbes.com/sites/forbescommunicationscouncil/2023/01/13/how-to-identify-your-businesss-target-audience/?sh=37f3c5ec789b

White, C. (2022, November 10). *What's a competitive analysis & how do you conduct one?* Hubspot. https://blog.hubspot.com/marketing/competitive-analysis-kit

Zhou, L. (2024, May 14). *2024 side hustle statistics: The ultimate list.* Luisa Zhou. https://www.luisazhou.com/blog/side-hustle-statistics/

ABOUT THE AUTHOR

Jason is a qualified Certified Public Accountant (CPA) and an entrepreneur. He has extensive experience in working with entrepreneurs across diverse industries, ranging from hospitality to construction. His professional background has provided him with a deep understanding of the intricate workings of various business landscapes.

Jason knows the challenges firsthand, faced by those on the path to success. Motivated by a strong commitment to small business development and entrepreneurship, he is dedicated to empowering new entrepreneurs by sharing his expertise and guiding them in building robust enterprises.

Jason's mission is to inspire and enable individuals to realize their dreams, equipping them with the tools, knowledge, and strategies necessary to navigate the complexities of business ownership. He aspires to foster a community where dreams are nurtured, businesses thrive, and aspirations transform into remarkable achievements.

Through his book, Jason imparts invaluable wisdom and practical advice, aiming to provide a down-to-earth, pragmatic resource to help business owners build their enterprises. He looks forward to hearing about the successes that readers will achieve.